Once Upon a Town....

The Story of Lakeville, Ohio

Copyright 2018 by

Cheryl Fields, Mary Tipton, and Shelly Spade

All rights reserved. No part of this book may be reproduced
or transmitted in any form or by any means
without written permission from the authors.

ISBN 9781731303295

For all the wonderful people of Lakeville, Ohio, past and present.

CHERISHED MEMORIES

The little town I desired to flee when I was so, so, young

Has now become cherished memories that I reflect upon.

Not a care in the world, for we felt safe to venture all around

Early morning, dark of night, during summer or on frozen ground.

I remember back yard camp outs, Good Lord we were so loud!

Waking up to dew damp sleeping bags if we ever slept at all.

I recall lots of neighborhood kids met at night for Kick the Can.

I swear we played for hours till we could no longer stand.

I remember in the winter when there was lots of snow,

We met at Rush's hilltop with sleds all in tow.

Piling all on one sled to see how fast we could go

Veering sharply at the bottom to avoid the huge tree in the road.

I'll never forget behind the school there was endless hours of play.

And we were all unsupervised, unheard of now days.

Swinging from the maypole, spinning high up in the sky,

The only thing that kept you safe was the ability to hold on tight.

Wednesday night we all gathered at the little Lakeville Church

For we had to practice with Doris for the choir Sunday morn.

I know all parents' spare change went directly up to Bud's

For pop, candy and comic books, that little bar I dearly loved.

I remember all the neighbors seemed to take us kids in stride

As we strolled through their tended yards, sometimes creating mischief

For which now I apologize.

I have to shout a thank you! Blessed little town

And all the ones I grew up with and for those no longer around.

Thank you for the memories!

C.W. Fields 5/19/2018

ACKNOWLEDGMENTS

Many people have provided us with great history and stories about their lives in Lakeville. Without your participation, this book would not be possible or, to say the least, a lot less interesting. And for that, we thank you. A special thanks to Becky Moyer-Darr who had the dream of writing the history about Lakeville and the special people who lived there. She got the ball rolling by compiling a large amount of information and pictures. Becky has a long history with Lakeville as she is a fourth generation originating from the little town. Her Great Grandfather Corwin Tope, Grandfather John Tope, and her mother Mary Tope-Moyer were all born and raised in Lakeville. We would like to thank Becky for passing the writing of this book to us as she had unforeseen circumstances that prevented her from continuing with the project.

Although this book has taken us a while to complete (we all have full time jobs), it was a rewarding project. Working as sisters was a great bonding experience. Extra time was taken to collect information and to formulate the lay out. Much investigating was also done for this book. Information was taken from personal accounts that spanned through many years and although all attempts have been made for accuracy, some historians may have different accounts of the subject matter.

 We hope you enjoy reading this book as much as we enjoyed writing it!

Table Of Contents

1.	Lakeville Demographics	7
2.	Who Was Mohican John?	13
3.	Lakeville's Early Beginnings	15
4.	Charlesburgh	21
5.	The Railroad	23
6.	Shoup Cemetery	29
7.	Ice House Business	35
8.	Lakeville – The Recreation Area of the Midwest	41
9.	Other Hot Spots	55
10.	The Sherman Brigade Reunions	59
11.	The Naughty Side of Lakeville	61
12.	Lakeville Businesses	63
13.	Lakeville Speedway	89
14.	Lakeville and the 1969 July 4th Flood	93
15.	The Great Blizzard of 1978	99
16.	Lakeville Schools	103
17.	Lakeville United Methodist Church	119
18.	Lakeville Post Office	123
19.	Lakeville Fire Department	125
20.	Lakeville Organizations	129
21.	Sports	133
22.	Lakeville Tidbits	135
23.	Lakeville Families	139
24.	Lakeville Homes of the Past	171
	References	177

1

Lakeville Demographics

The little village of Lakeville is located in the north-west corner of Holmes County, Ohio, along State Route 226 and west of O'Dell's Lake. Located in Washington Township, this little village is so small that we had a saying "don't blink or you'll miss it." There are no traffic lights, no town cop, heck, it's not even incorporated. In spite of this, there is a church, school, fire department, a few small businesses, a post office, and a rich history.

In the late 1800s, Lakeville was a booming place. Trains brought tourists in for fun on the lake. There were thriving businesses, stores, saloons, an amusement park, and hotels. Lakeville served all ages young and old.

Lakeville is located in the Glaciated Plateau Region of Ohio. This area has some of the most dramatic landscape in the area. The Glaciated Plateau also bears the most natural resources: gravel, sand, salt and coal. It also left behind some of the most fertile soil for farming.

The land in and around Lakeville is blessed with rolling hills and rich soil, great farm land due to the receding glaciers. The last glaciers to affect Lakeville were the Wisconsin and the Illinoisan. It is said they were a mile thick. They were so heavy they carved the hills and valleys. These glaciers originated in Central Canada and spread south covering approximately one-half of Holmes County before receding.

Lake O'Dell is a Kettle lake formed as a result of the glaciers. Three large pieces of glacier broke off while receding, forming this lake. It has three basins. The first basin is largest but most shallow, the second basin is smaller and deeper. The third basin is at the most western part. It is the smallest but also the deepest at 30 feet and is ½ mile wide. O'Dell's Lake received its current name back in the early 1800s when King Henry VIII had land holdings in America and granted the land to his royal ancestor, Thomas O'Dell. The picture on the previous page is The College of Wooster geological survey of O'Dell Lake and clearly shows the three basins.

Lakeville was first thought to be inhabited by the Paleo Indians (Ancient Indians) who were part of the Clovis tribe. It is speculated that they originated from New Mexico, as their artifacts have been found far and wide throughout the country. They were successful game hunters and foragers. They created the arrow heads that can still be found today in the newly plowed fields.

The Paleo Indians traveled up through the Bering Strait into North America during the Ice Age approximately 20,000 years ago when that area was above sea level. They traveled in nomadic groups following the seasons and the animals they hunted. They killed their game with stone and bone weapons. The Clovis culture lasted for approximately 500 years.

This is the actual photo of the excavation trench in the Quick Mound.- *from Holmes County Historical Sketches*

Following the Paleo Indians was the Archaic people listed in three groups: Adena, Hopewell and Fort Ancient tribes. These groups are responsible for the creation of the numerous earthen mounds. Three of these known mounds are located in Washington Township. Many mounds that may have existed were destroyed by land development and farming, thus destroying ancient artifacts that could have shed some light on their culture and survival.

There are two known mounds near Lakeville in Washington Township (and probably more than we will ever know). They are called the Quick Mounds. They were located on Isaac Quick's farm land. In 1820, Thomas Quick and Daniel Priest opened the mound and found deer bones, charcoal, a perforated stone with a picture of a bird scratched into it and some copper articles. (Holmes County Historical Sketches by Holmes County Historical Society). In 1880, a team from the Ohio Archaeological Society excavated the mounds. In the lowest mound nothing was found. In the larger higher mound, they found a burnt floor, pottery fragments, burnt bones, and a skeleton with about 40 beads around the neck. According to an article by H.B. Case, most of the artifacts crumbled when exposed to air. The surviving artifacts were donated to the Smithsonian Collection. H.B. Case also kept some of the treasures for his own collection. It is reported that Daniel Kick, who lived close to the Quick farm, drained his pond and found numerous flint instruments that were also donated. An unknown ancient mound was found southeast of O'Dell's Lake on land owned by J. Cannon. It was excavated by Dr. Boden from Big Prairie, where he found human remains. Further excavations or information concerning this mound is unknown.

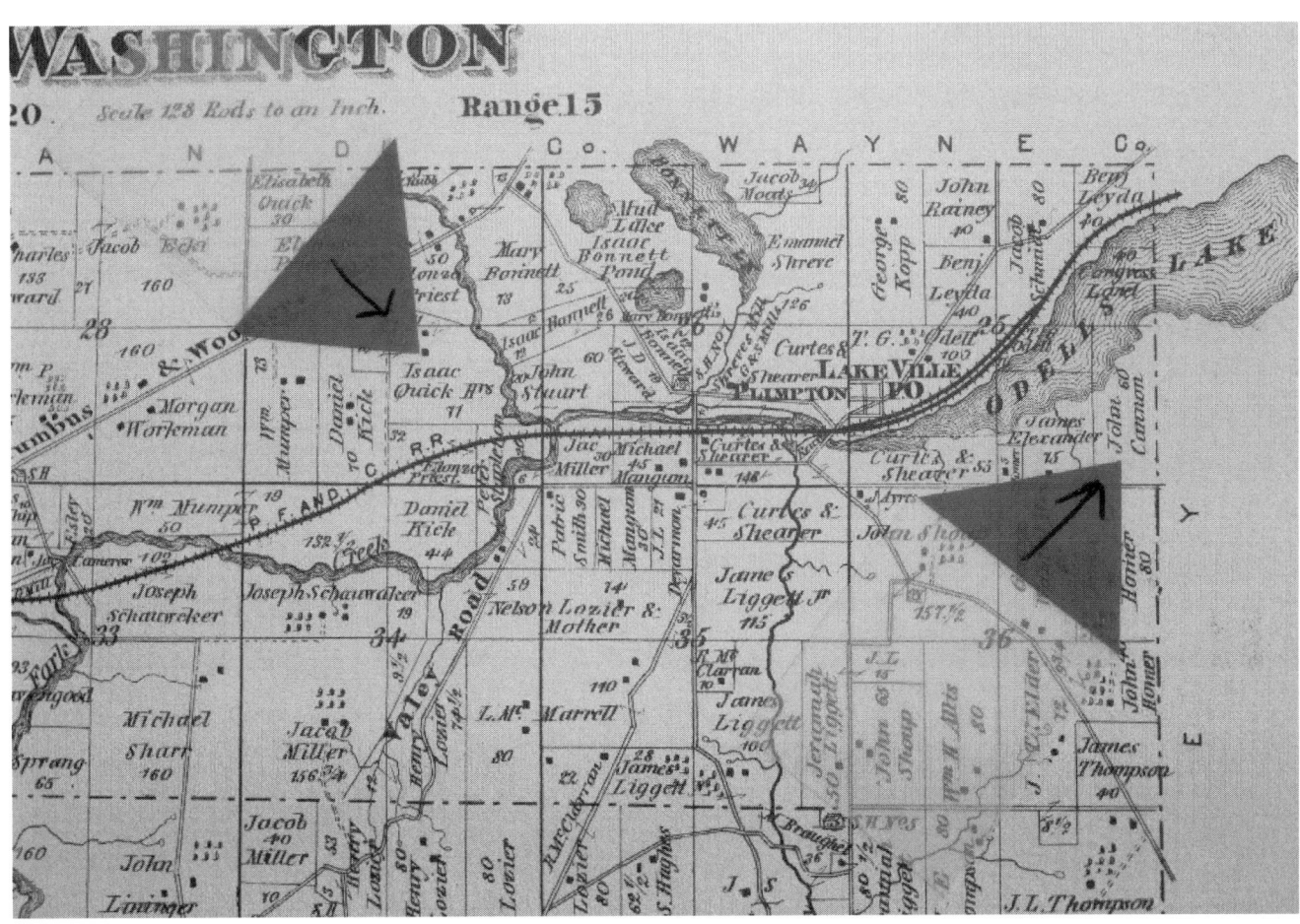

This map from the 1875 Atlas shows the location of the Quick and Cannon properties. The Quick land was located near the joining of the Lake Fork River and Crab Run. It is presently owned and farmed by Larry and Nancy Lorentz. John Cannon owned 60 acres on the southeast side of Lake O'Dell, bordering Ripley Township on the east side and road 511 on the south side. That property is now split into many lake side plots. The bulk of the former Cannon property is now owned by Linda Bush and Daniel Flinner.

After the Mound Builders, it is said that Native American tribes such as the Erie, Delaware and Pequot Indians inhabited the region. In the early 1700s, the Mohican Native Americans began to arrive to the Lakeville area. It is believed they traveled from Connecticut. Trading stations were developed. One of these trading stations was on the north side of Lake O'Dell. They called this Mohican Johnstown and it is said that there were approximately 300 Native Americans living there at one point in time.

We certainly cannot forget to talk about Johnny Appleseed and the fact that he came through Lakeville and planted several apple orchards in the area. One orchard was located where Crab Run and the Lake Fork River meet. There was another one located near Bonnets Lake (Long Lake) and one on the south side of O'Dell Lake. These original trees are now long gone as they only survive about 100 years.

Johnny Appleseed's real name was John Chapman and he was born in Massachusetts in 1775. He had a sister who lived in Mansfield, Ohio. In the early 1800s he began traveling with bags of apple seeds that he gathered from cider presses in western Pennsylvania. He traveled by canoe down the Ohio River and into the contributory rivers and streams. He would make stops along the way, preparing the land and planting the seeds. When the trees were saplings, he would exchange trees for clothing and other necessary goods. He did not sell trees for money. It is said that he was reclusive and lived in the forest. He was also a vegetarian. And, yes, he did wear a pan on his head and nothing on his feet, even during the winter. The Indians called him "The Medicine Man" as he taught them the medicinal qualities of herbs.

He took care of exhausted horses that were left to die and nursed them back to health. He was a very religious and caring person, spreading the word of God, love, and, of course, apple seeds. Johnny Appleseed died in 1847. My sisters and I did spot a few apples trees at the Mackey residence and they say that these are descendants of his trees.

Curiosity caused my sisters and me to take a walk along the tracks before fall was in full affect. We had three goals; see the Quick Mound, find an apple tree and perhaps cross paths with Bigfoot.

We ventured down the railroad tracks from Lakeville Memorial Park following the west rails. I must confess that I have never been down that way. It was absolutely beautiful. I now know why Ohio is called the Buckeye State, as we found several trees along the tracks. The old Quick farm is located at the junction of Crab Run Creek and Lake Fork River. We were hoping we would be able to just look across the fields and see a mound, but no such luck. We also had no luck finding the apple trees that were from Johnny Appleseed plantings. And, it was probably a good thing that we missed Bigfoot because three middle-aged women running back to our cars with wet drawers would have been uncomfortable and quite the sight! Even my sister's Bigfoot whoops

didn't stir the creature. Like I said, the scenery was beautiful! The old black majestic railroad bridge over the river painted a tranquil scene as the water babbled into the woods.

2

Who Was Mohican John?

Who was Mohican John? Was he a Native American or a white trader? Was he just a fable or a real flesh and blood person? Was he an individual or several people mashed up with several stories and legends to create one mythical persona? Not much is known or documented about Mohican John but let us look at all the stories attributed to him.

Myth: There are notes written by Eleanore Marmet-Thompson whose Grandfather Regne owned the property and Hotel from 1906 to 1934. Lake O'Dell was known as Mohican John's Lake. He was supposed to have been a white trader who had been captured by Indians and his name later became Chingagook.

Fact: Chingagook was a Mohican warrior who is a fictional character in a book written in 1826 by James Fenimore Cooper titled The Last of The Mohicans and a recurring character in Cooper's books, The Pioneers and The Leatherstocking Series. The books are set during the French – Indian Wars. Although

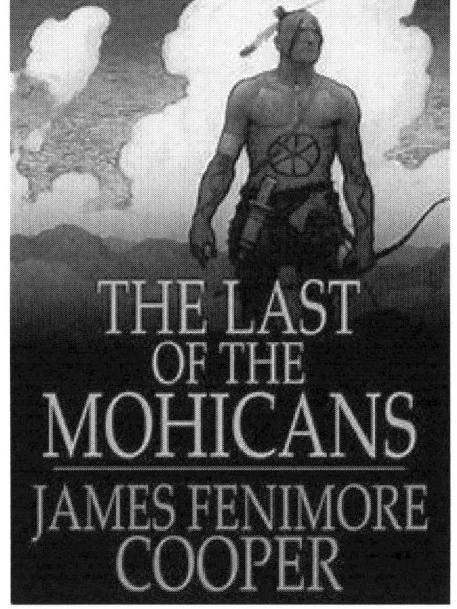

you often don't hear much about the Mohicans, because, although they were respected Indian warriors, they enjoyed a long history of perhaps misguided friendship with the British and later the American Colonists. Mohican Indian scouts served with Roger's Rangers in the French and Indian War and later fought alongside Colonial forces against the British in our war of independence. But they ultimately lost their lands in New England and New York and hence their dispersal and subsequent disappearance from history. Ultimately most of the remaining Mohicans, called now by their Christianized name, the Stockbridge Indians, settled and still live in Wisconsin.

Myth: Mohican John was a white trader who built a small town on the north side of Mohican John's Lake (now called O'Dell's Lake). John lived with the Mohican Indians who made him chief when he married a native tribeswoman.

Fact: Unknown, in my opinion I highly doubt that an Indian tribe would make a white trader their chief, although he has taken a native bride. Another story goes that, although the Mohican tribes were not known from this area, when the original surveyors came up the Clear Fork River plotting maps, they met a single native named John who was Mohican. The Mohicans began migrating west and some did settle in the area around 1760. When most of the Mohicans left, their relatives, the Delaware Tribe, moved into the area. Unfortunately, little is known about Mohican John, but it is certain that he was from the Mohican Tribe because in the mid to late 1700's, his name was well recognized by Native Americans and settlers in the region. For many years, a large Indian village was established in the area of present day Jeromesville by the Mingo Tribe under the leadership of Chief Mohican John, and the village was known as Mohican John's Town. The tribe also established the village of Mingo Cabins a mile northeast, on the east bank of Jerome Fork.

3

Lakeville's Early Beginnings

The first Colonial settler to lay claim to the Lakeville area was Isaac Newkirk. He was a scout under Colonel Crawford's command. In 1782 he obtained 1,000 acres between Bonnett's Lake (Long Lake) and O'Dell's Lake. He built a sawmill. He and his sons eventually built homes for their families after the War Of 1812.

The town of Lakeville had a rocky birth. The little town almost didn't happen and its name could have been very different. Back in the early 1800s, a man by the name of John Riddle had a dream. It was for the birth of a new town. He bought land from Isaac Bonnett. The land started at Lake Fork River and ended at Mud Lake (Round Lake). It was on United States Road which is now State Route 3. This area was also called Colliers Crossing. The land was comprised of 46 lots and there were four named streets: Wood Street and Sherman Lane (East

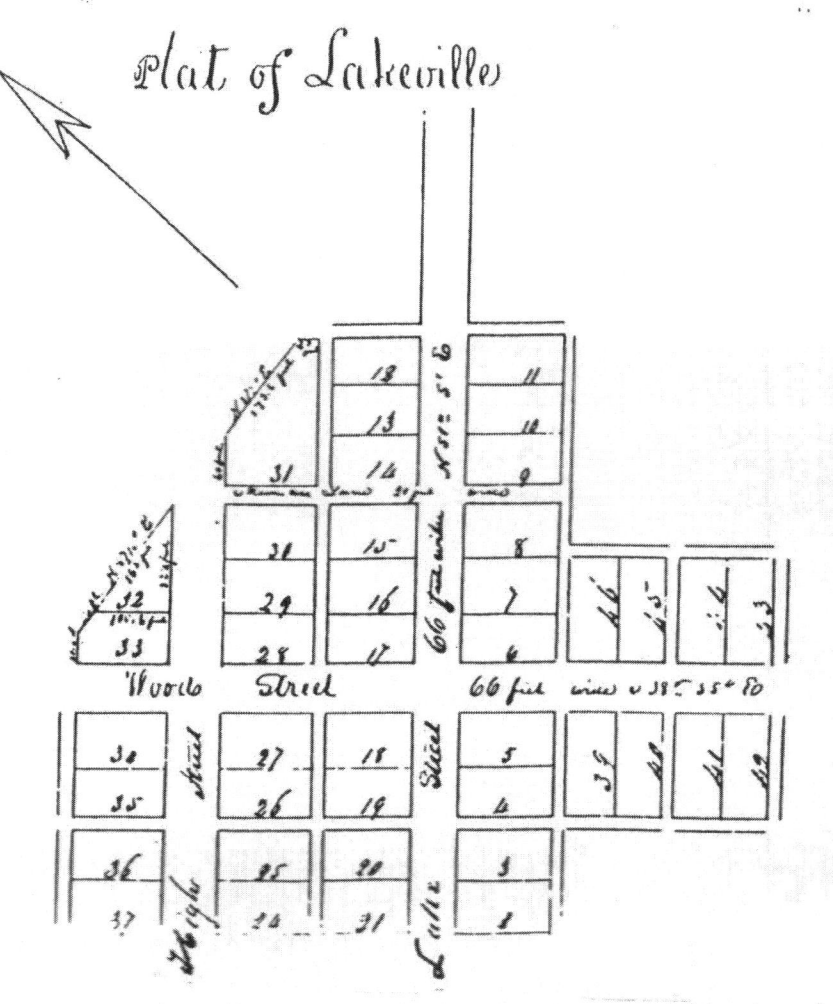

to West), Lake Street and High Street (North to South). At one point in time the (Old) Lakeville had a store, hotel, one room school, and several houses.

During the era of the town's birth, so also came the development of the Pittsburgh, Ft. Wayne, and Chicago Railroad. The railroad traveled west and east close to O'Dell's Lake. The sales of Riddle's land tanked and he sold it back to Isaac Bonnett in 1845.

Due to better shipments of grains, goods, and opportunities, the people began settling land around the lake and railroad. This land was owned and sold by the Plimpton family. The Plimpton daughter desired the town to be named Plimpton and the post office went by this name until July 3rd 1910. Considering that the town was between three lakes, there was a Thomas Lake who owned land on the west side, and the depot stop was called Lake Station, the name Lakeville evolved and stuck.

EARLY MAPS OF "NEW" LAKEVILLE AND WASHINGTON TOWNSHIP

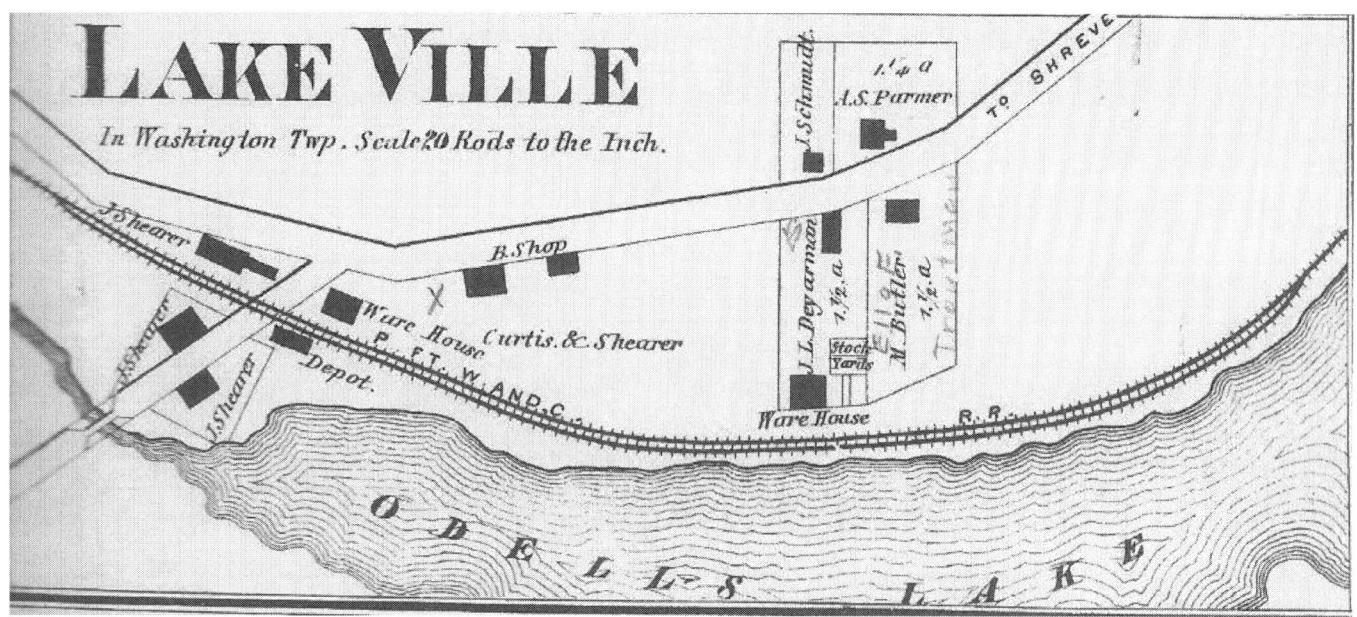

Map of Lakeville - *Caldwell's Atlas of Holmes Co. Ohio 1875*

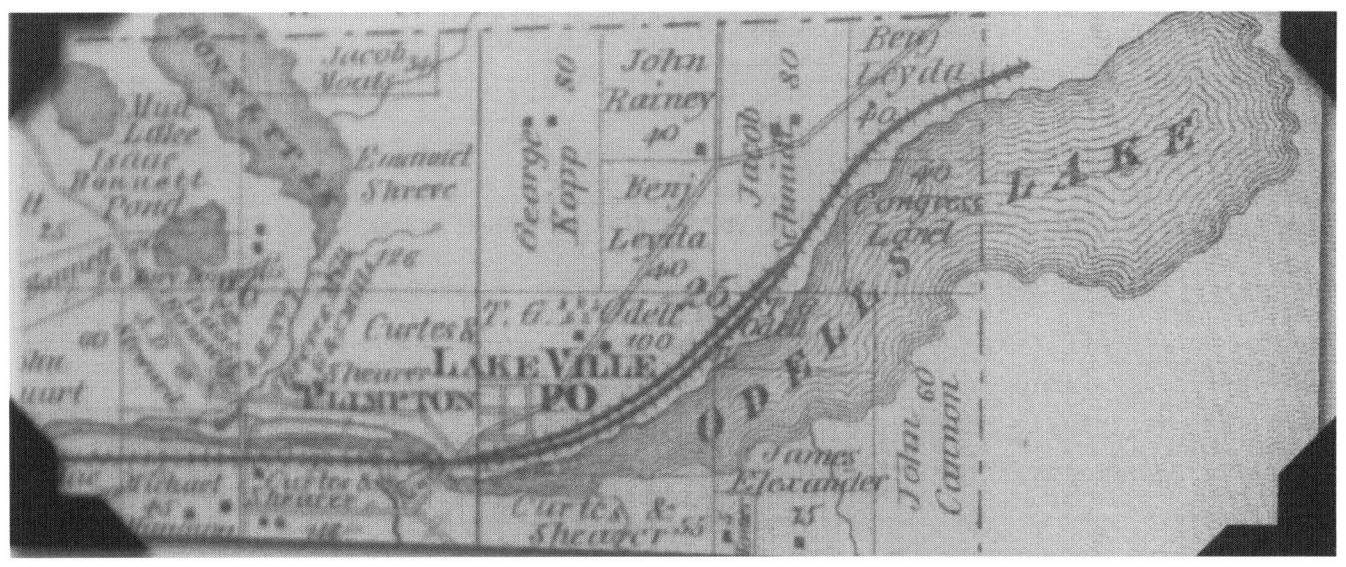

Map - *Caldwell's Atlas of Holmes Co. Ohio 1875*

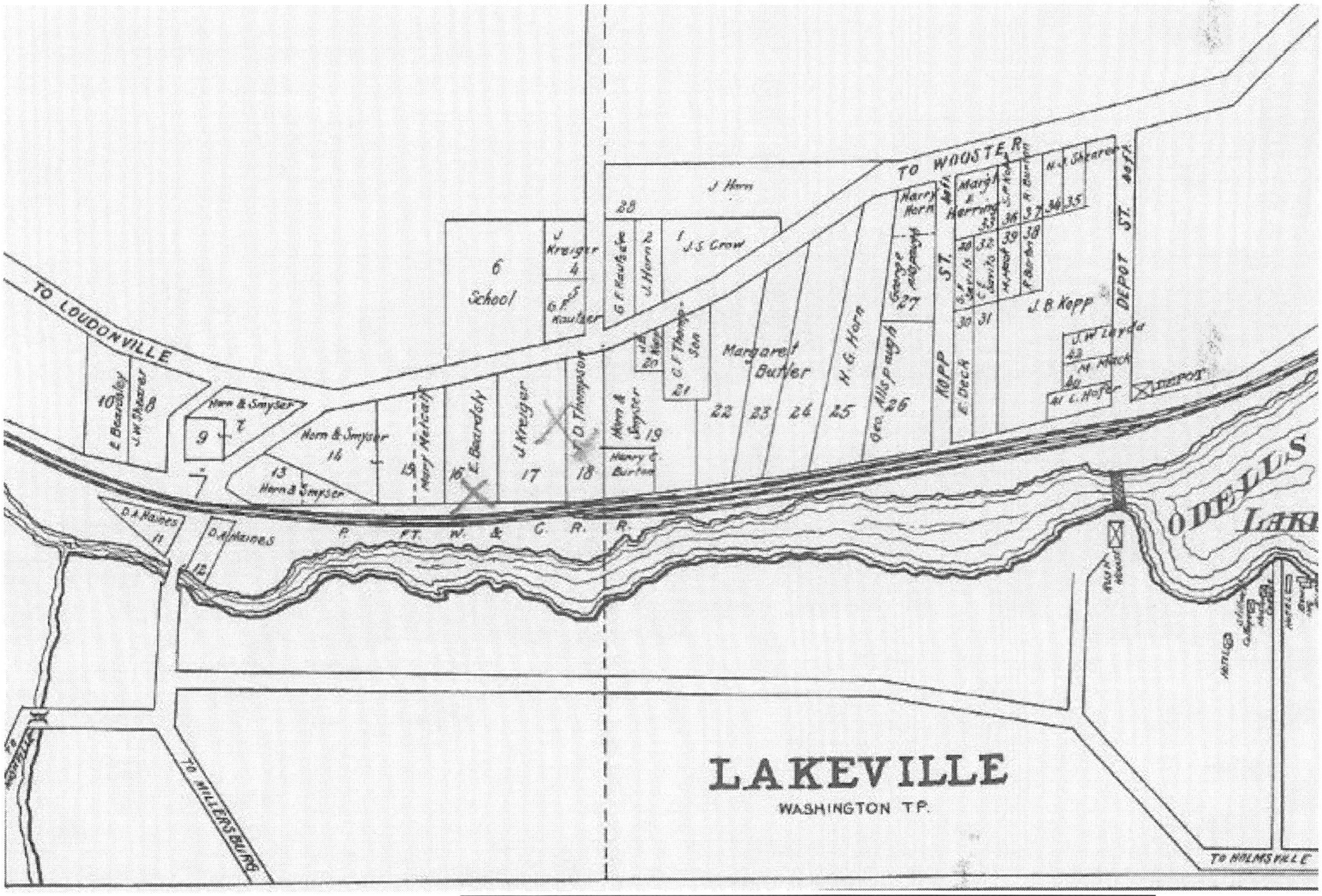

The Standard Atlas of Holmes County Ohio by A. J. Stiffler 1907

Map of Washington Township from Caldwell's Atlas of Holmes Co. Ohio 1875

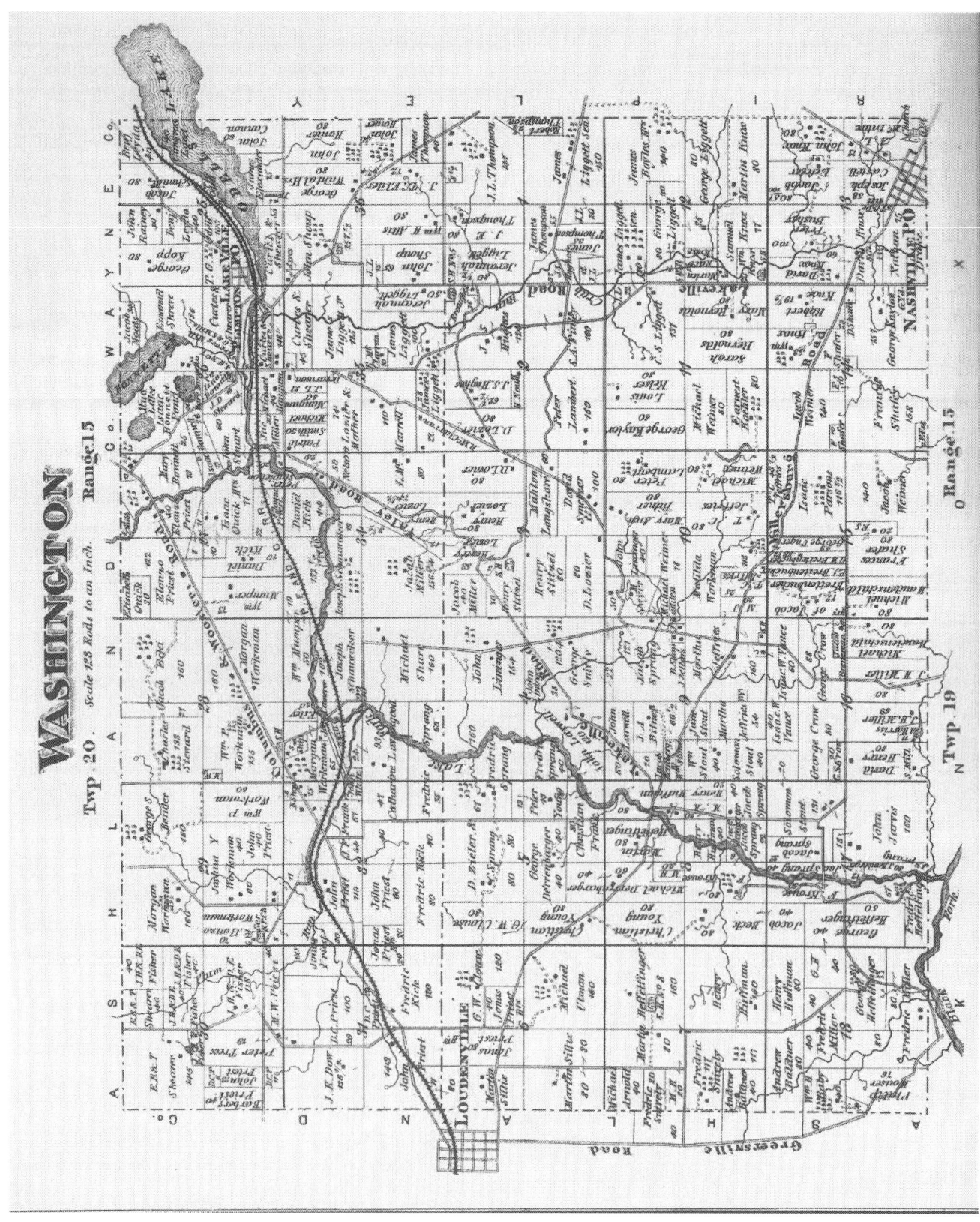

Washington Township – The Standard Atlas of Holmes County by A. J Stiffler 1907

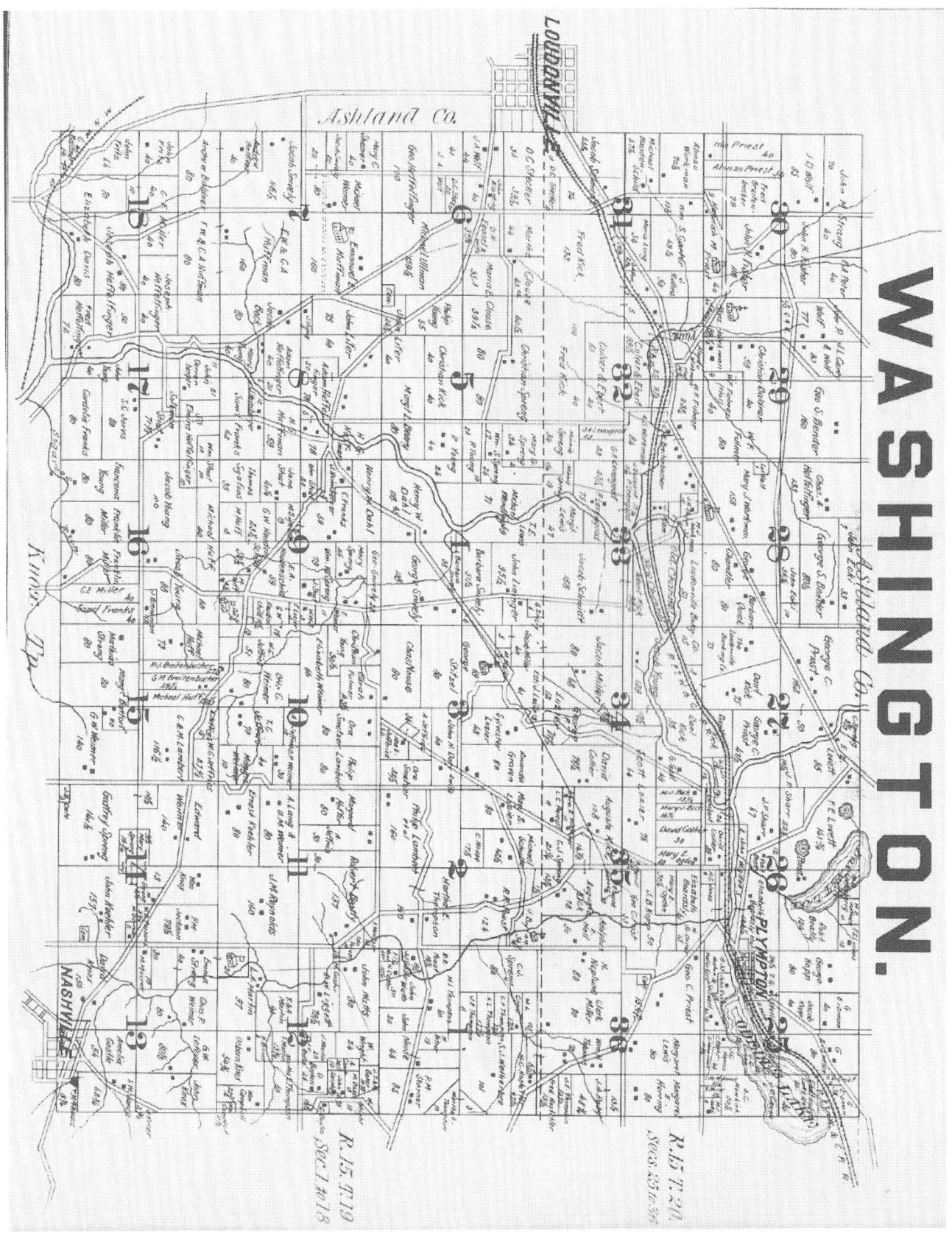

4

Charlesburgh

A Town That Might Have Been

A half mile south of the present-day town of Lakeville, nothing marks the former site of Charlesburgh, a town abandoned before it even got off the ground. In June of 1834, Charles Robison recorded a plat for a town in Washington Township before Justice of the Peace, John Shearer. Mr. Robison owned land at the Southwest corner of the Northwest quarter of Section 36, which is the intersection of Washington Township roads 470 and 472. Charles had Samuel Robinson survey a town of 32 lots. Set in a square, it was divided by two streets, one named North and the other Broad. No lots sold the first year but in 1835 – John Joyce and John W. Dowell purchased lots. The following year, Jacob Batdorf bought a lot – then Robert Justice and Thomas C Bowel. By 1841, several other lots had sold to Moses Stow, George Joyce, Jacob Burker, Thomas Liggett, and Stephen. The following year only one lot was sold, that to Michael Reed. Then, in 1843, James W. Riddle bought 4 lots. However, although no suit could be found in Common Plea, the State of Ohio took possession of the remaining unsold lots.

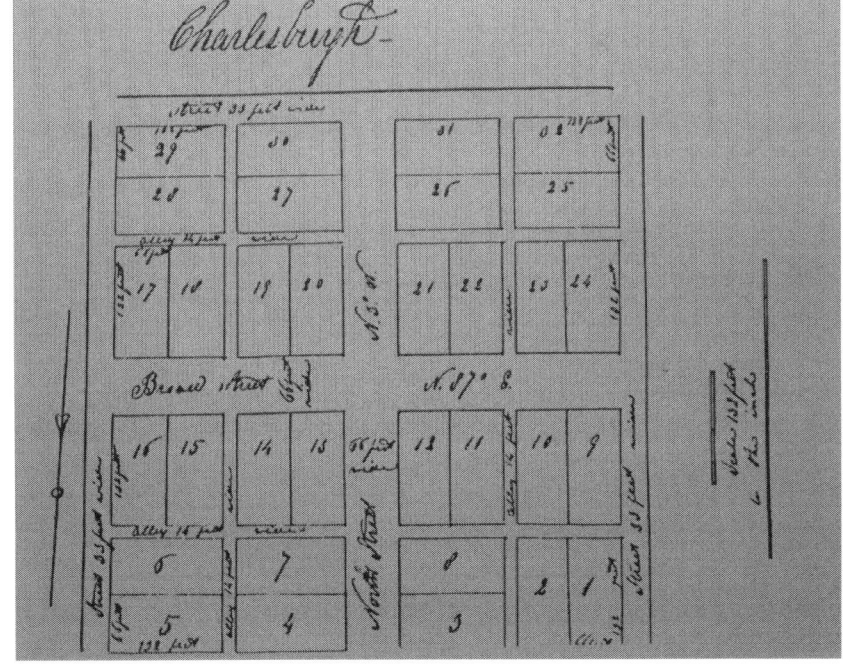

Perhaps Charles Robison had not paid his taxes. The story of Charlesburgh ended in 1844. In that year, John Shoup bought the land from the various lot owners and Charlesburgh was no more. Today, this area has only a small cemetery, Shoup Cemetery, to mark its location just south of Lakeville.

5

The Railroad

In 1848, the Ohio & Pennsylvania Railroad started to purchase land around Lakeville and the former Charlesburgh. Rails and a small steam engine were moved to Mansfield and the railroad was started, with the first line arriving in Lakeville in 1851.

In 1853, a second rail was installed. The stop was then known as Lake Station. The original depot was near the equity on the west end of town. When a new depot was built in 1882, the original became an office for the equity until it later burned down. The new station was built on the east end of town down at the bottom of Depot Street which was a more convenient location to the hotels and ice houses. A water tower and pump house were built to accommodate the trains.

In the pump house was a telegraph office for the railroad. Because of the ability for steam engines to fill their tanks at the station, Lakeville was known as a "jerk-water" town. The term came from the motion of jerking the water up in buckets from the supply to the engine. The pictures on the left are the train station as viewed looking down from Depot Street. The right-hand picture is from in front of the station, looking east towards Big Prairie.

According to the old Loudonville newspaper, the first freight and passenger train did not make it to Lakeville until 1854. When the rail line was finally completed to Chicago, the name was changed to the Pittsburgh, Fort Wayne, and Chicago division of the Pennsylvania Railroad.

The railroad also purchased land for a right of way from Elizabeth Newkirk. Elizabeth's son-in-law was Tobias O'Dell, one of the station masters. He owned the farm on the north going east out of Lakeville, currently owned by Porters. He had a son named Hal. They had a dairy on their farm. To the right is a wooden coin advertising the dairy. It was recently for sale on Ebay.

One railroad that never went anywhere was the Calico Railroad. One investor was John Spreng. It was to be located from Lakeville to Mount Vernon. The construction was contracted in March of 1853; however, only several miles of bed were completed. With the addition of the second rail to the nearby Lake Station that same year, work came to a halt on the ill-fated railroad. The workers were paid in calico cloth; hence, Washington Township Road 273 became known as Calico Road. The railbed was abandoned and sold in 1857 for taxes at a delinquent tax sale by the treasurer of Holmes County.

Many people are not aware that Lake Station played a role in a small skirmish during the Civil War. In Glenmont, located at the opposite end of Holmes County, local draft registers were opposing the Conscription Act (the draft). In June of 1863, President Abraham Lincoln sent General Burnside and his troops to Glenmont to settle the rebellion. Burnside and his troops disembarked at Lake Station and marched from there to Glenmont. It was the most notable anti-draft event to occur in Ohio. A skirmish was fought on June 17, 1863, between the Union troops and the local draft registers. The rebellion fizzled out, and became known as The Battle of Fort Fizzle.

The Lakeville, Ohio, Train Wreck

The following article appeared in the New Jersey Cranbury Press on March 7, 1890.

BURNED TO A CRISP

A Fatal Disaster on the Fort Wayne Railroad.

Three Lives Lost and $100,000 Worth of Property Destroyed.

A wreck that caused the death of three men and resulted in the destruction of property valued at $100,000 has occurred on the Pittsburgh, Chicago, and Fort Wayne Railroad, near Lakeville, Ohio. The names of the victims are: JOHN COWAN, engineer, Alliance, Ohio; HARVEY GALTHOUSE, fireman, Alliance, Ohio; and EDWARD MILLER, brakeman, Marshallville, Ohio.

Freight train No. 93 was running in several sections, and at Lakeville the third section broke a coupling, and the detached portion of the train, consisting of a dozen cars and three tank cars filled with gasoline, came to a stand. The conductor and brakeman of the third section said they at once started back to warn the fourth section. They ran for half a mile, placing many torpedoes on the track. But the warning was not heeded and the train, running down grade at the rate of thirty miles an hour, crashed into the third section, ploughing half through the detached portion.

As the collision occurred, the tank car exploded with a noise that could be heard for a mile away, and, the blazing gasoline spreading, the wrecked cars were soon enveloped in flames.

The three men who were killed were in the cab of the engine of the fourth section. Their bodies were burned to a crisp in the flames that raged for two hours. Oil and gasoline cars, gondolas loaded with coke and coal, and boxcars filled with merchandise made up the trains, and all this mass was fuel for as fierce a fire as ever raged after a railroad wreck.

The flames rolled up for a quarter of a mile along the track, and night was changed into day. Awakened by the explosions of the tank cars and alarmed at the fierceness of the fire, farmers hurried to the scene of the wreck from every direction. No one could approach within a hundred yards of the burning mass, however, and the charred bodies of the victims were not taken out for several hours. So intense was the heat that the bell of the engine to section No. 4 melted and the metal was encrusted upon the boiler.

The trainmen of section No. 3 say those of section No. 4 must have been asleep. It is believed, however, the warning was not as timely as these men claim.

A report from the March 6, 1890 edition of the Democratic Northwest newspaper stated that the wreck occurred just west of Lakeville around 1:00 AM.

The Stark County Democrat, on March 6, 1890, gave a graphic description of the victims: *The remains of Engineer Cowan were found some distance from the track against a clay bank. It was reported that he was asleep on his engine, hence he did not see the signal to stop. The finding of the bodies in such a position showed that all the train men jumped for their lives. What was left of poor Galthouse was gathered and put in a dish pan.*

Legend has it that the wreckage of the train was buried near the equity.

Another train mishap occurred in April of 1935, when the draw bar on a pusher engine snapped. A caboose and three cars landed in Lake O'Dell in front of the railroad station. Three men were injured in the incident: J.D. Bullas of Canton, fractured ribs; E.D. Beechy of Alliance, broken legs and ribs; and Jones Easily of Alliance, scalp injuries.

Concrete foundation of depot as seen from railroad track.

Passing train as seen from depot foundation.

With the demise of the Lake O'Dell resorts and the ice business, the Lakeville Depot was eventually closed and torn down. The building's concrete foundation is still visible at the bottom of Depot Street.

The following poem was written to commemorate the passing of the railroad station.

The Old Depot   -   Author Unknown

For seventy years, it's patiently stood
Serving the people as best as it could.
In summer and winter, sunshine and rain,
It sheltered the people for the coming train.
A platform of wood stood outside the door
And the boards inside were warped on the floor.
But 'twas a friendly old building sitting there,
Housing the old, the young, and the fair.
It greeted the first train that came down the tracks
With its dinky engine and funny smoke stack,
When there was only one track for all the freight,
For locals and passengers and for old Number Eight.
If it could talk, what stories it could tell
Of trips and journeys and excursions as well,
Of Grandpap and Grandma and other folks, too,
That courted while waiting there for old Twenty-Two.
It would tell of the lake so placid and cool
With fishes a-plenty, the fishers to fool,
Of picnics that were held in the old shady grove
Just over the outlet this side of the cove.
But today came the word of the saddest kind.
The friendly old depot has met Father Time.
Tho' its years of service were nearly fourscore,
The verdict of man has just closed its door.

In October of 2017, Kevin Williard gave a presentation about Big Prairie Church Camp at the Ken Miller Museum in Shreve, Ohio. Following the presentation was a question and answer session. The following tidbits were offered up. I have not seen anything in writing to substantiate these statements, so I pass them along as word of mouth, not confirmed facts. In the early days of railroads, there were Christian and non-Christian railroads. The original Pittsburg railroad was non-Christian. For a train to stop, a town had to meet certain standards, including have a depot, hotel, and at least one house of ill-repute. The Pennsylvania Railroad was a Christian railroad and would place Pullman cars containing chapels on rail extensions. It was also stated that, in general, throughout the United States, Wyatt Earp and Bat Masterson controlled the railroad prostitution.

Today, the railroad is back down to one set of rails. The concrete box pictured to the right is all that is left of the former pump house near the former depot. The box contained the water pump.

6

Shoup Cemetery

Located at the same site as the ill-fated town of Charlesburgh, near the intersection of TR470 and TR472, you will find Shoup Cemetery, sometimes known as Lakeville Cemetery. It is named after John Shoup, who bought up the various lots of the ill-fated town of Charlesburgh. When we visited, the landscape crew was just finishing their mowing. While the grass was very well kept, the tombstones in the  cemetery were in sad shape. Over the years, whether due to Father Time, Mother Nature, or vandals, a lot of the smaller monuments have been broken. The broken stones have been placed in neat piles throughout the cemetery

While wandering through, as with many old cemeteries, we found many markers for small children. One particular heartbreaker was inscribed: "Hear (sic) lays five infanc (sic) of

Cornelius & Margaret Quick." It was propped against Margaret's grave. She lived from 1798 – 1876. I'm happy to report that, when returning to the cemetery several months later to take some more pictures, I found that the Quick infant gravestone had been placed somewhat upright alongside the stones of their parents.

On the web site FindAGrave.com, there are 107 recorded memorials. The earliest listed is 1831, Roland G "Rola" Puffer, and the most recent is Delbert Carter in 1957.

According to the book, Holmes County Veterans, found at Millersburg Library, among the veterans buried there are George Wachtel, 1795-1866, who served in the War of 1812. Civil War veterans are Horatio Johnson, William HH Liggett, Nelson S Lozier, and Isaac (Dr.) Wiggins. It is also said that there are several Revolutionary War soldiers buried there. Shown on the next page are the veteran graves that have markers and flags. It is interesting to note that those who served in the Civil War might have different markers. Some have the one marked "Civil War" while others have markers with "GAR" on them. The GAR stands for The Grand Army of the Republic and was a fraternal organization composed of veterans of the Union Army, Union Navy, Marines, and the U.S. Revenue Cutter Service who served in the American Civil War for the United States forces.

31

I was able to locate a few of the veterans listed above and several additional ones.

Jeremiah Liggett – Civil War

George Wachtel – War of 1812

Nelson Lozier – Civil War

Isaac Wiggins – Civil War

Marcus Knight – World War II

7

Ice House Business

One of the biggest businesses in Lakeville was the ice houses, owned by the Consolidated Ice Company of Pittsburgh, operating from 1870 until 1926 when the ice business was abandoned due to the invention of refrigeration by electric. John Rush Jr. operated and managed the two ice houses located on the north side of O'Dell's Lake near the railroad depot. The business employed approximately one hundred people.

The ice houses were so well insulated, that when one ice house burnt in 1907, the ice inside was only melted on the edges due to the heavy insulation of sawdust, rye grass, and hay. Over fifty thousand tons of ice was stored and shipped each year and four railroad cars were loaded each day during the winter for deliveries to other ice houses along the route in the towns of Crestline, Mansfield, Wooster, Canton, Massillon, Alliance, and Pittsburgh. Businesses and homes depended on ice deliveries for refrigeration and passenger trains would stop and take on ice for drinking water.

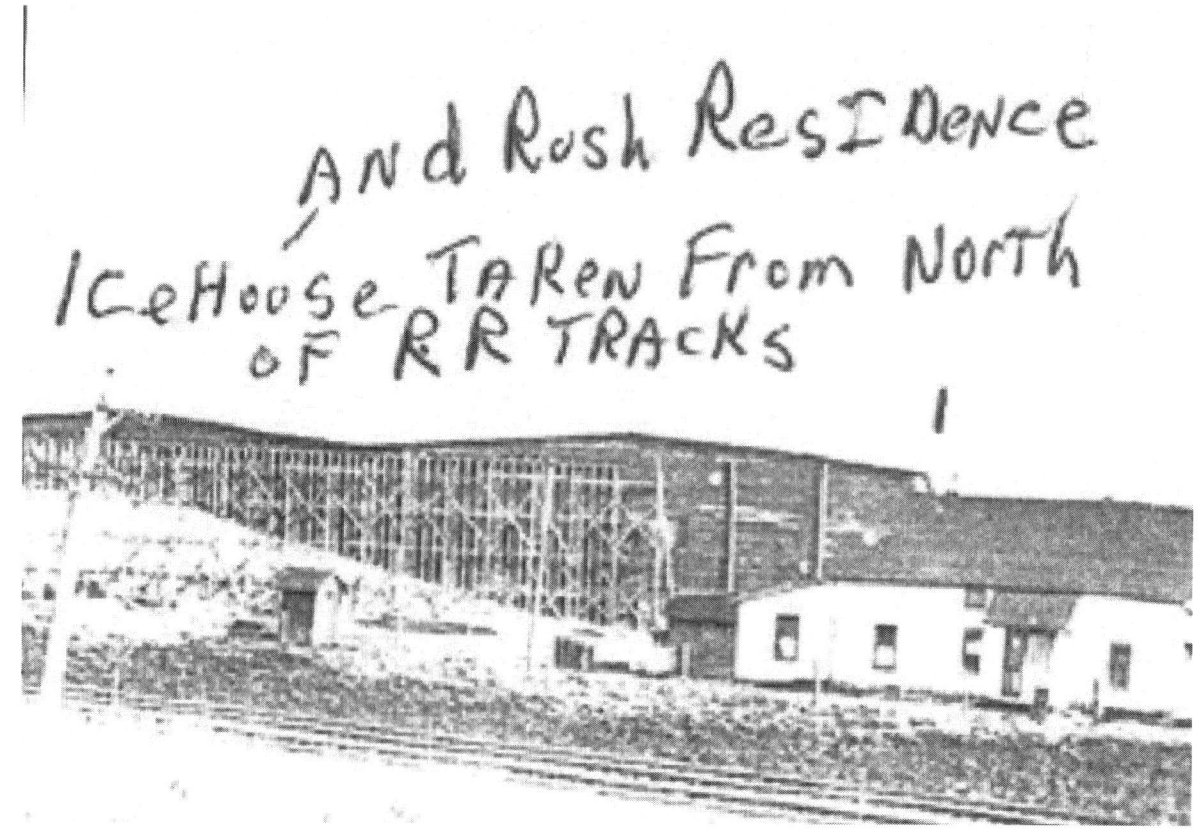

Icehouse and Rush Residence taken from north of RR tracks

CUTTING THE ICE

Ice cutting was not only an art form, but a well thought out choreographed procedure. First, straight lines were cut with horse drawn plows that had teeth like a skate. Four inches of ice was always left underneath the ice field for safety reasons. The plows went both directions cutting the blocks of ice which were then floated and fed up the elevator to the ice house. The ice was split into a two-inch thickness before going up the elevator and being stored. There was another elevator on the other side to load rail cars.

Many thanks go to Brooks Harris and his family, who, before his recent death, granted us written permission to publish pictures from his and wife, Kathleen's, book *Holmes County, Ohio – History in Photo Postcards.*

The ice cutting operation at Lakeville in the early 1900's was run by John Rush, Jr. With the coming of electricity, the ice business folded and put 100 men out of work.

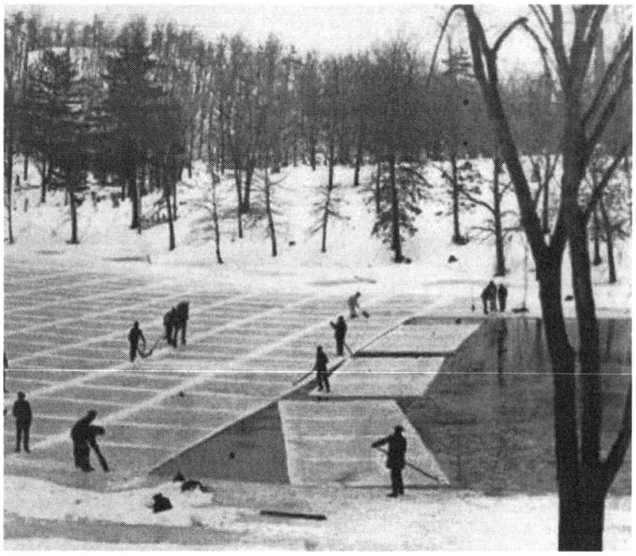

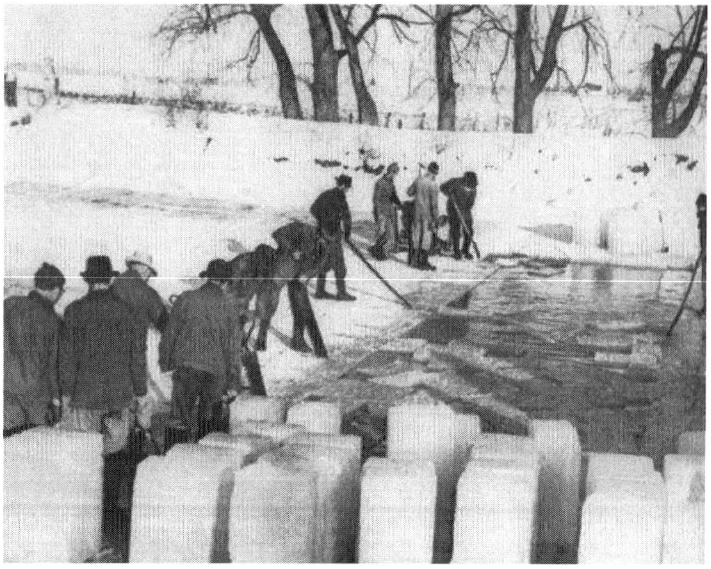

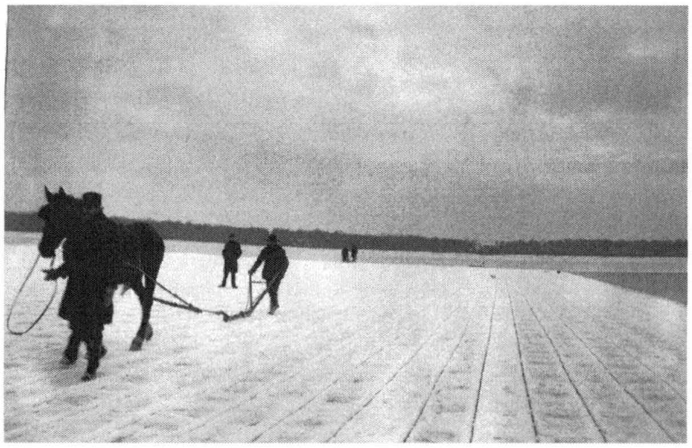

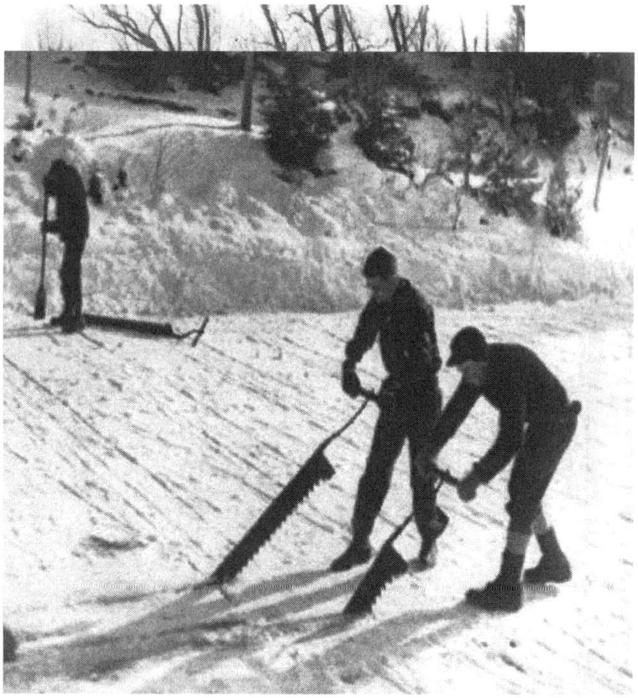

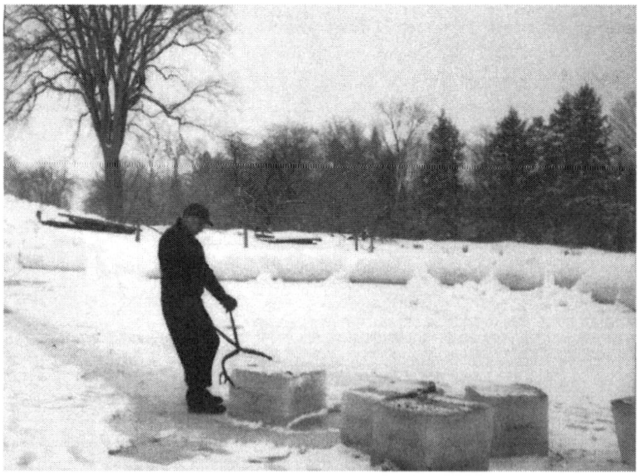

J.L. Regne and K.Q. Rush shown with the horse drawn cutting plows they used for cutting ice on Odell's Lake.

HARVESTING THE ICE

8

Lakeville – The Recreation Area of The Midwest

When you pass through the current sleepy little town of Lakeville, it is hard to imagine that this little burg was once a thriving community supporting a train station, hardware store, hotels, grist mill, ice house, restaurants, grocery stores, a buggy shop, warehouses, blacksmith, a school and church. But what Lakeville is most known for is that O'Dell's Lake was known as the Recreational Area of the Midwest during the 1880s to 1930s. People came from all over Ohio and as far away as Pittsburgh. Because of the easy railway accessibility, this area rivaled Geauga Lake which was built the same year. There were three amusement and recreational areas at different times from 1870 to 1965.

Grand hotels were built around the lake. First there was the Lakeview Hotel and grounds built by John Rush Sr. around 1870 on the west end (Lakeville end) of the lake. The hotel was a four-story structure with fifty rooms. The hotel was operated by Jules Regne, who eventually bought the hotel from Rush in 1906. Later the hotel was renovated to a two-story building, renaming it the Lakeville Summer Resort in 1910. Rush Sr. also had built cottages that people could rent out for their weekend excursions.

The hotel's first floor was on ground level with an open covered concession counter for refreshments and an open porch. A saloon/bar, common

41

gathering room, dining room and kitchen were also situated on the first floor. On the south side of the first floor facing towards the train tracks was a wash room with five or six mirrors and sinks. This made an easy access to the public outhouses that were built over the outlet that ran eventually into Crab Run Creek and Lake Fork River. There were six to eight "stations" and everything went into the water. People said it was not too bad as long as the wind and water went downstream.

The second floor of the hotel hosted a stage for the bands and a ballroom that doubled as a skating rink. The upper floors had long hallways with sleeping rooms on either side and bathrooms located at the end of the hall on both floors.

The hotel grounds also hosted camping, boating, fishing, swimming, picnic areas, and dances. The Rushes had built a special sail boat to transport the band. The band was from Nashville, Ohio, and they would play melodies that would drift across the lake. There was also a steam boat that would take people around the lake. Rush also built a fleet of rowboats, each named after one of his children. There was also a bandstand area and dancing pavilion. From 1930 to 1965, there was Oak Grove Park located on the south side of the lake near the west end, offering swimming and picnic areas. It was owned by Lloyd Horn, who also owned a hotel on the hill behind it.

Rush's Lakeview Hotel

Pictured above and below is bridge from train depot to the hotel area. Picture to the right is how it looks now.

Dick Porter remembers using the bridge to deliver newspapers when he was young.

Cottages at O'Dell's Lake

43

Boat Landing and Hotel, Odell's Lake, Lakeville, O.

Bathing Scene, Odells Lake

Boating Scene, Odells Lake

Refreshment stand at Lakeview Summer Resort

Picnic Grove, Odell's Lake, Lakeville, O.

Lakeview Park was a popular resort area.

LAKEVIEW PARK RESORT

Holiday gift / advertising plate from C. L. Rush – *from the collection of Bob Walters*

Lakeview Park token – *from the collection of Bob Walters*

Swimmers at Lake O'Dell – *photo courtesy of Rex Parsons*

47

Aerial view of southwest side of Lake O'Dell near where the hotel once stood. *Photo courtesy of Lyle Gray*

48

ODELLS LAKE LAKEVILLE O

PARK AT LAKE VIEW SUMMER RESORT
LAKEVILLE O

Lake View Park
on
Lake O'del

South Side of Lake
South Cty Rd 100

50

Lake View Park on Lake O'dell

Both pictures are of George Wigton swimming at Lake O'Dell. Picture on right shows hotel in background. – *Photos courtesy of Lynn Wigton Baker, George's granddaughter*

Lily Patch, Odell's Lake, Lakeville, O.

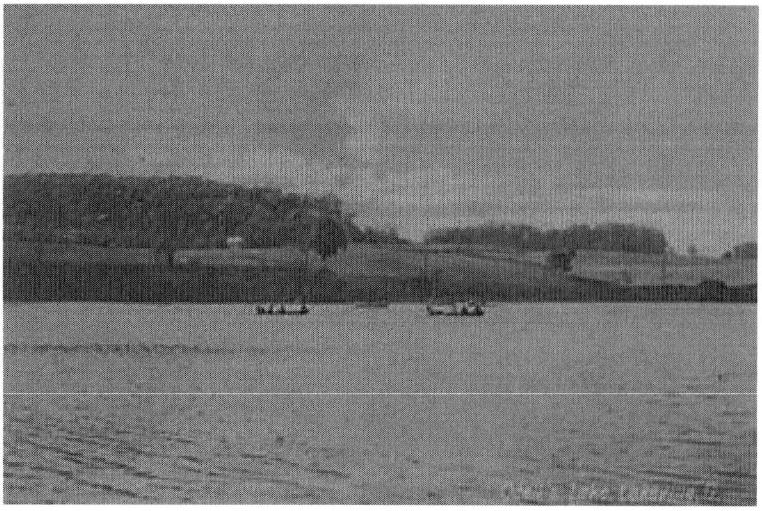

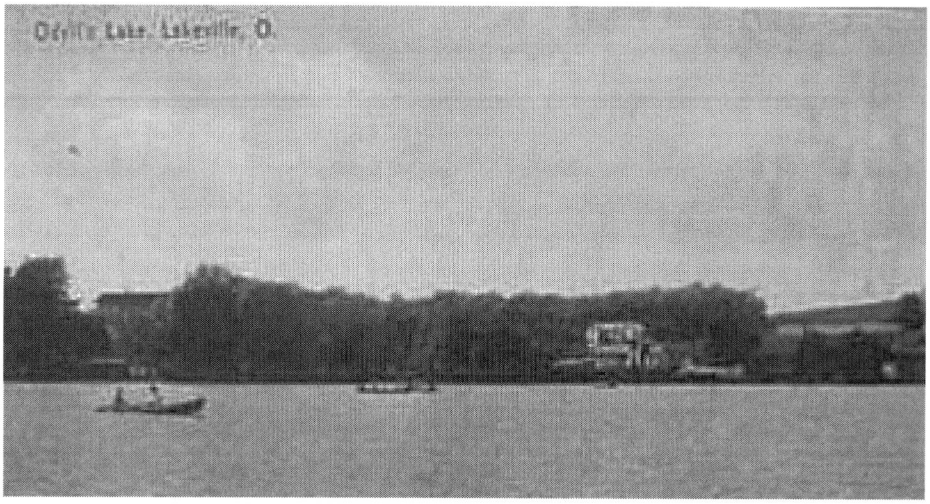
Odell's Lake, Lakeville, O.

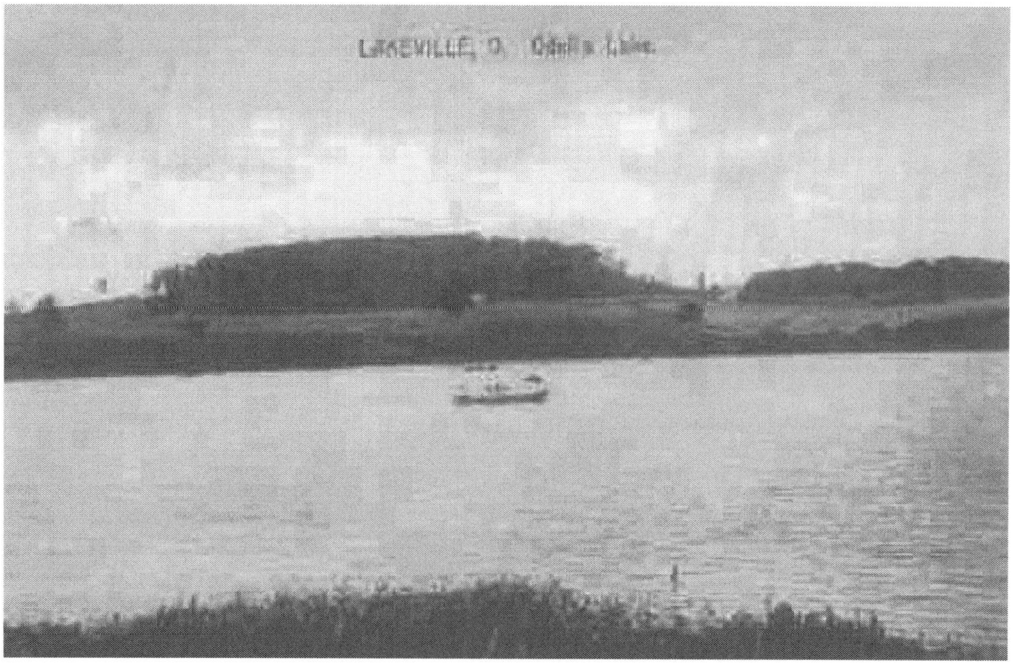
LAKEVILLE, O. Odell's Lake.

9

Other Hot Spots

Lakeland Beach

An amusement park was located at the east end of the lake at the Lakeland Beach Area owned by John Lake, boasting a bandstand, roller skating rink and dance hall, Ferris wheel, carousel, miniature train and a rollercoaster. There was also a ball diamond that featured The Bloomer Girls from Chicago who played there often. Sometimes there would also be a circus entertaining guests and visitors to the area. John Lake also added a bath house and an inground pool around 1911. He was given permission to build a road on that side of the lake, thus completing County Road 100. The park was open from 1922 to 1940. Some of the amusement rides were sold to Chippewa Lake when Lakeland Beach closed. Some of the rides still sit today on the abandoned site of Chippewa Lake Park, but lack their original beauty. Some of the Lakeland Beach photos are courtesy of Kevin Williard.

Swimming pool under construction

Lakeland Beach bath house under construction

Lakeland Beach BATHhouse About 1930?

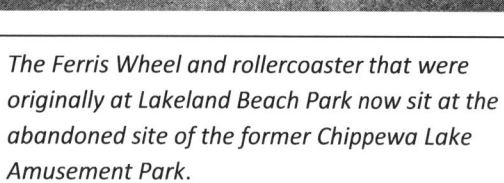

Lakeland Beach BAThhouse

The Ferris Wheel and rollercoaster that were originally at Lakeland Beach Park now sit at the abandoned site of the former Chippewa Lake Amusement Park.

Train ride at Lakeland Beach Park – *photo courtesy of Kevin Williard*

Long Lake

Long Lake is also a Kettle Lake formed from the glaciers. In its early years Long Lake was known as Bonnetts Lake after the owner, Isaac Bonnett. A campground was established in

Long Lake Park 1930's.

A LONG LAKE BATHING BEAUTY IN 1908.

1919 and it was renamed Long Lake.

This campground is still in operation and is the oldest campground in Ohio. The campground is comprised of 62 acres of land and the lake is 60 acres. I remember swimming in the lake as a child but now they have a heated in ground pool and the lake is used for fishing.

Long Lake Park 1950's.

10

The Sherman Brigade Reunions

Although General Sherman's troops never served in the Lakeville area, the annual reunion and encampment of the Sherman Brigade was held at O'Dell's Lake. All counting, eight annual reunions were held at O'Dell's Lake. I am not sure what specific years they were held, though I do know that a reunion was held on the grounds in September of 1885. This is probably the first time and the last time that Lakeville made the New York Times. It was reported that over four hundred soldiers were expected to attend the reunion, being as they served under General Sherman from Chattanooga to Atlanta. The brigade was made up of veterans from the 64th and 65th, O.V.I. (Ohio Volunteer Infantry) and McLaughlin's Squadron. The organizations served in the Armies of Ohio and the Army of Cumberland from 1861 to 1865. Tents would line the land on the west end of the lake and the troops would have drill exercises and mock battles. Close to seven thousand people would come and watch the brigade perform these exercises.

> **THE SHERMAN BRIGADE REUNION.**
> MANSFIELD, Ohio, Sept. 3.—At the reunion of the Sherman Brigade at Lakeville yesterday Gen. Sherman and Senator John Sherman were present. In the afternoon a crowd of not less than 6,000 or 7,000 persons listened to addresses from the distinguished guests. Senator Sherman's speech was an eloquent and effective review of the causes, events, and results of the war, and closed with an appeal to the patriotism and fidelity to the Union of the children of the heroes of the war. At the conclusion of the Senator's address Gen. Sherman was introduced and gave the veterans of the brigade one of his characteristic speeches. His address was fatherly and affectionate in tone, and his touching allusion to his advancing years and rapidly approaching end profoundly affected all present.
>
> The New York Times
> Published: September 4, 1885
> Copyright © The New York Times

General Sherman began his fighting career at the First Battle of Bull Run, serving under General Ulysses S. Grant. Sherman later succeeded Grant as the Union Commander of the Union Army and captured the city of Atlanta.

Sherman's most well-known campaign in the civil war was "The March to the Sea", or more commonly known as the "Savannah Campaign", conducted through The State of Georgia from November 1864 to December 1864. The campaign began with Sherman's troops leaving the captured city of Atlanta in November 1864 and ended with the capture of the port of Savannah in December 1864. Sherman's forces devastated military targets and civilian businesses.

Union soldiers also freed many slaves, who in turn helped the Union soldiers while on the march. When trying to join the Union Army near Savannah, many African Americans drowned trying to cross Ebenezer Creek, located north of Savannah.

11

The Naughty Side of Lakeville

In its early booming days, 1870-1930s, Lakeville was well known for excitement, fun and relaxation. Families had Lake O'Dell with its surrounding Parks, one park even had amusement rides. You could listen to the band that floated on the lake and watch baseball games. There were hotels with numerous amenities including roller skating rinks and slot machines. Lakeville was known as the entertainment capital of the Midwest. With all this wholesome family fun, Lakeville also had to have a naughty side.

It is reported by Glenn Kaser, who resided on County Rd 100, that his former home used to be called Rosie's and was said to have been a red-light district house. It is reported that prostitution was common in the area and that when cars and electricity arrived to Lakeville that prostitutes from surrounding counties would flow in for some undercover business. They would also get away from the law. They reportedly stayed in some of the cottages around the lake. It is reported that there could have been at least 30 of them down by the lake at one time

During the prohibition years, 1920-1933, Lakeville didn't have to worry too much about not having booze as there were 6 stills and 17 bootleggers around Lake O'Dell. Some of the bootleggers were Yaky Shultz, Raymond Weaver, Snapper Newman, and Ma Rider. Mort Reed said that he used to ride with Sheriff George Marks around Lake O'Dell and that one day they stopped to talk to one of the still owners. The sheriff was informed that the still had been out of working order for a month because of a burned-out coil. That nice sheriff went to town and returned with a new coil so the operator could get back into production. There was also plenty of homemade beer and wine made by the locals in Lakeville to keep many lips wet in those days. After prohibition was ended it is said that the East side of the Lake (around Big Prairie) continued to be dry but the west side (Lakeville area) was as wet as a waterfall.

According to Lisa Ferris Miller, a story was told to her by her family that when her Aunt Viola worked as the switchboard operator in the old Wagner home, that Pretty Boy Floyd stopped in to use her phone after riding in on a train.

A "dance hall", actually a cover up for a "Speak Easy" called the Castle Inn, was supposedly built by mobster Herb Hewitt. It is also said that Frankie Sunday lived next door and often frequented the establishment. Castle Inn was located on the south side of County Rd 100 and Township Rd. 508 (Crow Hill).

The infamous Castle Inn

12

Lakeville Businesses

During the writing of this book, many times we have wished that we could get into a time machine and travel back to the heydays of our home town, when Lakeville was a thriving, self-sufficient hub of activity, the entertainment capital of the Midwest. As with many small towns, the invention of electricity and automobiles dealt a blow to the local businesses. The birth of refrigerators ended the need for the ice business. With the production of automobiles, blacksmiths and carriage makers became obsolete. If you had a car, why would you visit your local hardware or general store when you could visit the "big cities" and shop there?

This chapter describes the many businesses that have come and gone over Lakeville's history and a few that are still around.

THE 1800s

Around the time that the railroad came to Lakeville in 1851, three business were built across the railroad tracks near the west end of town. They were a railroad station, a saloon, and an equity.

The railroad station was run by Wilbur Wolf. However, wanting a station that was nearer to the lake, resort hotel, and ice companies, it was replaced by a new station on the east side of the town in 1882. The old station was then used as the office of the equity until it burnt down.

The equity was also run by Wilbur Wolf. Near it was a saloon that was built and ran by George Gaul, who also built the first house in Lakeville. The saloon went out of business in 1919 and became part of the mill for the equity. Cyrus Quick constructed a grist mill further up the inlet from the equity around 1848.

Located on the opposite side of the railroad tracks, coming into Lakeville from the west, the first building on the right was a blacksmith shop.

Next to the blacksmith shop, a store was built in 1850. It was ran by William Wolf. After 1860, a hotel was added to the store, making it the first hotel in Lakeville. George Gaul ran it in the 1880s, with John Shearer taking it over in 1892.

Around 1848-1850, on the east side of the store / hotel, the first restaurant in Lakeville was owned and ran by Glen Nizely. Not much else is known about it until it changed hands to the Kellys in the 1900s.

Blacksmith shop – still standing at west end of Lakeville.

Also, on the west end of town, on the current site of Hamlin Racing Engines, Henry Curtis built a hardware store between 1849-1853. He asked Joseph DeYarman to run the store as DeYarman had experience running several other hardware stores. In 1864, DeYarman built a brick Victorian home located at the intersection of State Route 179 and Township Road 273. The home still stands there. The house is reported to have been part of the Underground Railroad during the Civil War and DeYarman's obituary states that he helped free 125 slaves. He also owned a prosperous race track diagonally across from the house.

DeYarman had a dispute with the Henry Curtis family and left the hardware store. He bought land located in the center of town, running from the road back to the railroad. He built a general store on a steep bank near the road. At the street level was a general store. The bottom level, accessed from the rear, was believed to be the location of his hardware store. At the back of the property, by the railroad tracks, he built a warehouse and stock yard. His son, Charles, ran this until 1895.

The DeYarmans were also in the banking business. During 1893–1897, there was a serious economic depression in the United States.

In 1895, the stock market crashed and the family lost everything, including the brick Victorian house.

After a short ownership by William Shipp, the DeYarman store in the center of town was purchased by Simon Kopp around 1896. Simon was born in Lakeville on December 4, 1876. He began clerking in a general store at the age of 15. He would have been around 20 when he conducted his own store. Various members of the Kopp family owned the store until the early 1940s.

Lakeville Adv. Business Directory.
PLIMPTON P. O.

Jacob Schmidt, Dealer in all kinds of Family Groceries, Tea, Coffee, Sugar, Tobacco, Flour, and everything usually kept in a Grocery Store.
Mrs. M. Butler, Hotel, Lakeville, Ohio.
C. S. Deyarman & Son, Dealers in Dry Goods, Notions, Groceries, Boots, Shoes, Queensware, Glassware, Clothing, &c., Lakeville, O.
J. L. Deyarman, Dealer in Grain, Seeds, Wool, Salt, Plaster, Fish, Lime, and Coal, Lakeville, O.

Businesses advertised in Caldwell's Atlas of Holmes Co. Ohio 1875.

In 1894, John W Horn moved to Lakeville. By 1898, he and partner, Ervin Smyser, opened a hardware store and grain elevator. It was located at the same site as the one owned by Henry Curtis, so one would assume they were one and the same.

In the 1870s, John Krieger opened a blacksmith shop and was also a buggy / carriage maker. The blacksmith shop and his family's home were located across from the present school building. It is said that his buggy business was conducted in the same building that later housed Cagle Manufacturing. That building is located several buildings to the east of the current school house. Or it might have been on property that Krieger owned behind the Armory.

RESIDENCE OF JOHN KRIEGER

Krieger Residence and blacksmith shop

Across from the Krieger residence, the Plimpton Guard Armory was built in the middle 1880s. The Guard served in the Spanish-American War and World War I. It was later used by the school for basketball games and class plays. It was also possibly used as a doctor's office or storage for Krieger's buggy shop. If you look closely at the picture, you can see advertising

on the front of the building for Krieger's shop. It also has the name Gerstenslager on the bottom line. The Gerstenslager Company, of Wooster, was also a manufacturer of carriages, so perhaps they had formed a partnership. The Armory was demolished in 1938 to make room for an addition to the Lakeville Special School.

The Armory pictures were provided by Shelly Spade. We believe they were given to our parents, Jim and Pat Walters, by Vera Butler. Note the Cities Service sign in the lower right-hand corner. This was a brand of gasoline at that time.

Located in the center of town, was a building that served three purposes. In 1896, at the age of 28, James Edwin Thompson and his wife, Coral, opened a store. The store, located in the middle part of the building, carried groceries, tobacco, cigars, and notions. The left side housed the residence. On the right side, was the town's first post office. Thompson was appointed Postmaster on June 2, 1897 by James A. Garey, Postmaster General under President McKinley. The Thompsons had one child, a daughter, born in 1896.

RESIDENCE OF JAMES E. THOMPSON

THE EARLY 1900s

The Holmes County 1907 Atlas contains the following:

Lakeville Business Directory

Lakeville is situated on the Pittsburg, Ft. Wayne & Chicago R. R. and is a thriving little village.

The Post Office is Plimpton.

Collier, David..................................Ex-Representative, Wool Dealer

Haines & Shearer..............................Grocery and Saloon

Horn, John..Grain Dealer

Krieger, John....................................Carriages

O'Dell, T. G......................................Station Agent

Rush, John Sen.................................Hotel and Saloon

Regne, J. L.......................................Saloon

There is one church in the village, a good school house, containing two rooms.

HORSE BUSINESS IN
PLIMPTON (LAKEVILLE).

D G Chandler also managed the Farmers Equity in the early 1900s

The Lakeville Equity was located across the railroad tracks on the west end of Lakeville. In 1925, it became part of the Loudonville Equity. Gretchen Tipton shared that she and her father, Blaine Greer, both worked at the Equity. Blaine was a manager there for many years and Gretchen worked there from 1977 – 1992, then moved to the Loudonville location. Many former residents remember visiting the store to buy feed for pets, or a pop or Yahoo chocolate milk. If you didn't want to pay for the bottle deposit, you could finish your drink there and then turn the bottle back in. Others remember digging through the piles of corn cobs in search of red worms to go fishing.

Above photo provided by Gretchen Tipton and taken by Dave Polen

Early 1900s picture of Equity – *photo courtesy of Bob Walters*

The former Lakeville Equity. Note – as of Jan 2019, the mill is in the process of being torn down

The Ralph Kopp family was still running their general store. Paul Kopp (1913–1984), their son, wrote an interesting account of his youth for his daughter-in-law, Rita Kopp. Rita gave us permission to print his article in our book. A few excerpts from that article follow.

Dad had a general store in a little summer resort town of about 150 souls. This was the eyes and ears of the whole rural township, boasting a railroad station on the Pennsylvania Railroad, a telegraph operator, and water tanks for the old coal engines.

Mother was the telephone operator, and the switchboard was installed in the kitchen of our house across the road from the store. Lakeville also had a restaurant and pool room, with the town barber installed in one corner. I well remember getting a 25-cent haircut and a front row seat at a pool match all at the same time.

Down the street a few doors was the blacksmith (John Krieger) *with his glowing forge and teams of horses waiting outside for their turn at a new pair of shoes.*

The door was always open, winter or summer, and you can imagine the wide eyes of the ragamuffins of 6 and 7 as they watched the shoes forged and nailed to the horses' feet. It was a special privilege if you were allowed to give the bellows a pump or two and watch the sparks erupt from the fire.

A few more doors down the street was the grain elevator and hardware store (Horn). *The wagons used to line up at threshing time to sell the wheat, which was often the only cash crop of the farmer.*

After the grain was weighed, it was dumped into small grain cars which were hand propelled across perhaps 50 feet of elevated rail and dumped into the elevator bins from above, and stored until the Pennsy had a boxcar to haul the grain away to the terminal.

Our chief joy was to jump perhaps 30 feet from the car rail into the bins of wheat below, then scamper back up the ladder to have another breath-taking jump.

I always liked the shipping room where feed was sold to the dairymen of the area. Open bags of bran and molasses-filled dairy feed filled my tummy quite often. If a cow could eat it, so could I!

We would also ooh! and ah! over the guns and knives displayed in the glass cases in the front of the store.

I heard the Dempsey-Tunney fight from a high bank across from the hardware. The hardware owner had just received a marvelous box which operated from a six-volt car battery and was called a radio. He set it up outside and played to a full house of local boxing fans in the makeshift theater.

There was another elevator across the railroad, too, but we stayed away because that was a co-op and supposedly evil for taking business away from the rugged individualist, my father being a "rugged individualist."

At one time there was a saloon across the railroad, but when I was 5 years old, the "drys" prevailed and prohibition reigned. We used to fish from the river bank behind the saloon and tell tales of the awful things that went on inside, of course influenced by the remarks of my Methodist mother.

Of course, when I was a teenager, we used to watch the local bootlegger surreptitiously hide his stock in trade down a groundhog hole and carefully cover it with leaves. After dark, we would borrow a pint, and just as carefully, replace the leaves.

It must have been a congenital compunction as great-grandfather (George Kopp Sr.), who was deaf, was run down by a Pennsy engine while crossing over to the saloon one afternoon.

On the opposite side of the road "downtown" was the local school, Lakeville Special, which was a forerunner of our modern consolidated schools. Newly built, it housed all the schoolchildren of the township, doing away with the one-room schools. It was very modern, taught all 12 grades and even had a high school basketball team which played in an old National Guard armory next door that had been abandoned.

Behind the school was the baseball diamond, a very popular place, for before football blossomed, baseball was a nine-months vocation for most kids of the town.

That baseball diamond was a bonanza too, for when it was graded, there were dozens of Indian arrow points unearthed. Our imaginations ran rampant!

My friend and I had a row boat in the lake outlet across the tracks, behind the store. There also was an old fellow who never worked but always had fish and meat on the table.

We would watch from a high bank at night as the old fellow would drop his fish traps up the outlet and into the lake. Before daylight, we checked out the traps to make sure he had no more than he could eat. We were well supplied too.

The summer time was a special time of joy for then the campers arrived at the resort by the lake. The Pennsy used to run excursions from Pittsburgh, and the place was hopping. Many people came from Mansfield, Canton, and other towns for a few days of good fishing and quiet restful nights.

Saturday night was dance night and the local beau brummels filled the floor with the beauties of the area and danced 'til 12 to the music of varied and sundry combos.

My special memory is of putting a nickel in the slot machine, legal then, of course, and hitting the jackpot of a hatful of coins. I never could figure why it never happened again.

My father was a musician, too. He often came home for lunch and practiced his violin until it was too late to eat and he went back to work. He organized a dance band of seven or eight and played round and square dance each Saturday night all the winter season.

He would take me along and while he performed, I would be having a ball with the other kids, ringed around the round oak stove, red hot with fire and music, too.

Saturday night, while Father bowed and tooted, Mother tended the store. The hitching rack was full of horses and buggies outside. We kids used to play hide and seek in and around the buggies, ducking in and out, under the horses' bellies, with no thought of danger. We had a ball as all was dark except for the store window.

The store was on a steep bank with the front at street level and the back door a story below.

I must tell you about my first sight of an airplane. After World War I, the country was full of barnstormers. One such fellow came to Lake O'Dell to take the locals a ride at $5 per 10 minutes.

People had talked about airplanes but I never thought I would see one. The whole town turned out to the cow pasture to see that marvel. Uncle Jacob was one of the lucky people who had $5.

Located behind Kopp's general store was a broom factory. It operated from 1902 to 1907, when it burned down and was not rebuilt. It was owned by George Kantzer and his brother-in-law, Jacob Kopp.

By 1906, J L Regne owned the former Thompson store in the middle of town. He converted the center area to a bar and restaurant. The right side was a barber shop and the left side remained the residence. His son-in-law, Cecil Marmet ran it for a while.

The hardware / grain elevator partnership of John Horn and Ervin Smyser dissolved in the early 1900s and John's young son, Harvey Kay, joined the business. A 1925 year book ad lists the business as J W Horn and Son. Pictured to the left is Horn Hardware. On the back of the picture was noted, by Mrs. Lloyd Horn in 1960, *"Horn Hardware and Elevator, Lakeville Ohio, Holmes County. Sometime before 1917. "Doc" Collier, J W (Dad) Horn, and "Oz" Knox in picture left to right. Timbers at left front are part of the support of old track to grain bins in the elevator building."*

The picture to the left shows the inside of Horn Hardware. J.W. Horn (left) and Harvey K. Horn (right).

In 1920, the hotel on the west end of town changed hands from John Shearer to Charles Ferris. Ferris was a janitor at the school and a barber. His wife was Mary Mamie Wachtel. An addition was added to the building for a telegraph office which was run by his daughter, Viola. The addition also housed Charles' barber shop. This property later passed to another daughter, Beatrice, who married a Wagner. Her son, Bill, is the current owner; however, the home is no longer habitable.

First hotel in Lakeville. Wagner home.

72

The following businesses were listed in a 1928 advertisement:

Lakeville is situated between O'Dell's and Long Lakes, both of which are fine summer resorts. Lakeview Park, at the west end of Lake O'Dell, is owned by J L Regne.

Our Farmers' Equity is under the management of George Wharton, he having succeeded D G Chandler, who resigned to take care of his insurance business. (Note: the Lakeville Equity Exchange Company became a branch of the Loudonville Equity in 1925.)

L R Burgett is busily engaged in heavy trucking, moving, hauling live stock to Cleveland, O., and all kinds of produce also.

John Krieger who has been engaged in blacksmithing and making wagons for a number of years in Lakeville, recently decided to quit. He is making a store room of his shop. When ready, Glen Horn will occupy the room with a fresh new stock of groceries and provisions.

D B Krieger, the Star Auto salesman and garage man.

R H Kopp, the old reliable grocery man.

Ferris and Wachtel, proprietors of restaurant and pool room. Also Mr. Ferris is our city barber.

Sharr and Crow, milliners with the latest in ladies headgear.

James Hudson is our obliging postmaster.

S E Rush is our local R R agentt; Roscoa Deitch our section foreman. Chas. Collier, Edgar Brennman, and Carl Parsons telegraph operators. Thos. Crow is our careful crossing watchman.

Our schools are under supervision of B F Feichter and assisted by his able corps of teachers, E S Glasgo, Dorthy Cooke, Mary Frank, and Mrs. G L Stevens.

J W Horn and sons carry a full line of hardware, feeds of all kinds, coal, brick and pay highest prices for grains.

There will be preaching services at Lakeville M E church Sunday evening. Rev. W M Freer, minister. Sunday school at 9:45 am. H J Butler, Supt.

A gas pump was added to Dudley Krieger's garage, located on the Krieger property, in the 1930s, selling the Cities Service brand of gas. If you look closely at the bottom right hand side of the Plimpton Guard Armory picture, you can see the sign that was in front. His mechanic was George Sprang, who worked there while going to school. The garage was torn down in the 1960s by Jim Walters and replaced with a two-car garage and workshop. A pipe which was used to fill the underground gas tank stuck up out of the ground near the garage. It was also removed by Walters after a neighbor girl, Mary Miller, tripped over it, requiring stitches.

The Krieger home was located next to the gas station. Later homeowners included Blake and Minerva Darling, Jim and Pat Walters, and Don and Patty Hudson.

Although, it wasn't located within the town of Lakeville, Fulmer General Store, pictured to the left, was within the Lakeville address. This was their delivery wagon. It was located in McZena.

THE MID 1900s

On October 20, 1933, Lakeville School Minstrels presented the play, "In a Garden of Loveliness." Ken Bauer provided us with copies of the program. The following businesses advertised in the program:

Dud's Place – Dudley Krieger's garage / auto sale

R. L. Pettit – Marl and Marl Products - Nature's Own Plant Food for Lawn, Garden, and Field

Horn & Wachtel – Groceries, Meat, and General Merchandise

Lakeville Dahlia Gardens – Dahlias of Quality and Merit

John W. Horn & Son – General Hardware, Elevator, Radio and Supplies

By the early 1930s, the Kopp General Store was in the possession of Miles S. and Helen (Horn) Wachtel. Helen was the daughter of John W. Horn, owner of the hardware and grain elevator down the road. A 1946 yearbook ad lists the store as carrying groceries, meats, soft drinks, candy, and Pace ice cream.

Meat Market

Becky Moyer Darr reminisces: "When I was a kid and Miles and Helen owned the store, I clearly remember Miles taking a piece of meat, putting it on the paper tore from the roll, and tied it so fast I never saw him tie the knot."

Harry and Mary Jones were the last owners of the store. It was purchased by the bar next door, and tore down for a parking lot in the 1960s.

In the early 1940s there was a butcher, Verdelance (Verd) Rush, located in a barn on Horseshoe Alley between Rhameys and Topes. On Saturday evening, February 20, 1943, Verd decided to make his way home to the other side of the lake by walking across the frozen lake. He had been in town purchasing groceries and getting his mail. He fell through the ice, and his disappearance was not reported for several days because it was felt that he would show up at his home after a few days. They had to wait until spring to dredge the lake and recover his body.

Posey's Place bottle opener – *photo courtesy of Bob Walters*

The restaurant / bar / barber shop changed hands several times in the early 1930s. Posey's Place is advertised in the 1931 yearbook. It was owned by Hipps in 1932 and then Joe and Frieda Bock bought it in 1935. They were from Germany and owned it for approximately 20 years. Frieda was famous for her "sizzled" cheeseburgers. Sometimes when they went back to Germany to visit family, Mary, Pete, and Becky Moyer would move into the residence portion and run the bar for them. Becky remembers that Joe always called her "Pinkie" because of her red hair. The Bocks had a son, John, who became a doctor in Columbus.

In 1933, Wayne Gray Horn, son of Harvey (Kay), graduated from Lakeville school and joined his father in the hardware and grain elevator businesses. Wayne enlisted in the US Army in 1942 during World War II. He served in Africa and Italy. He served as forward observer for the heavy artillery where he had emergency surgery, which brought an end to his army duty. He was sent back to Cleveland Veterans Hospital, discharged in 1945, and returned to Lakeville where he rejoined the hardware and elevator. Wayne took over as sole owner of Horn Hardware and Elevator and a tavern was added in 1946 known as the infamous "Horn's Bomb Shelter." It was located in the basement. The business was sold in 1949 and Wayne became a rural carrier and raised beef cattle and hogs. He, wife Alice, and mother Nellie Horn would become the owners of Horn Nursing Home in Wooster.

The Bomb Shelter was run by Kay Horn. It came with its own mascot, a cussing parrot. Becky Darr is pretty sure that Kay had something to do with that! It is said that a drunk tried to get the parrot to say "Polly want a cracker" and the parrot told him to go "you know where."

Marge Musselman shared a memory of starting her singing career there. She sang "It Wasn't God Who Made Honky Tonk Angels." Because she was underage, she told her mother that she and her friend were going to a movie.

The following poem about the Bombshelter was written by Mary Tope Moyer:

The Bombshelter

Going to the Bombshelter on Saturday night
Is like going to a dozen shows
Those who don't care for noise and commotion
Can take their business to 'Joe's
There stands 'Herb the Bartender' with bloodshot eyes
He drinks up all the profits while Al stands there and sighs.

No doubt the next person to come into view
Would be 'Dally' Huffman or 'Hoop Dee Doo'
Looking for pardners for 'Just one game'
If they said 'Let's play all night' it would mean the same

In comes 'Charlie My Boy' and whispers 'I've got a fifth'
Then half a dozen guys want to give him a lift
Above all the noise of moans and groans
You'll hear 'Tubby' Austin rattling his bones
(Then half the customers take off for Stone's)

A regular customer is little 'Bob' Hall
When it comes to tall stories he's right on the ball
He sits on two stools, he's too big for one
He's an eighth of ton of fat and fun

There's Frank Wachtel, hobbling on one crutch
It looks like he's had too much
Clarence Wachtel is here too, you can tell they're relation
When it comes to drinking beer they're both a great sensation

In walks 'Pete' Moyer followed by Frank Beck

I still think they deal from the bottom of the deck
Wendel Albertson come in all sharped up
Paul Graber sits there as meek as a pup
Blake Darling is present and so is his wife
Some drunk's in the corner reliving his life
Take another look, there's Mary behind the bar
You can tell by her expression that she's not up to par

Harold Gieogue says "It's the worst thing that ever happened to me"
Bill Snyder just got a good slapping for free
You'll hear 'Walt' Sigler calling Ruth 'Dearie'
His son Don and his wife discussing Einstein's Theory

There's Harold Jefferies and his wife Mabel
She wants him to go home while he's still able
Dick Gilliam is over there huddled in a corner
(I bet the story he's telling would shock Cliff Horner)

Hillbilly music resounds from wall to wall
If Bill 'Tennessee' Sours don't sit down soon, he will no doubt fall
'Mouse' Mosher will be here sooner or later
Some guy's pester Lorna trying to date 'er

Coleen comes in occasionally look for Herb
Sometimes it's just thirst she's trying to curb
The telephone rings, Herb pulls out his hair
He knows it's some woman, 'Is my husband there?'

Bud Sponseller comes in delivering Coke
Orry Stuhl sits there listening to some stale joke
Harve Harpster comes in with the cutest grin
(I bet he's not so cute without his false teeth)

The evening just wouldn't be complete
Unless Carl Everhart stomped on your feet
He'll stagger around and land in a booth
Then you'll hear those famous words "That IS the truth"

Lo and behold Kay has returned
Arriving from Florida all sun-burned
He rolled up his sleeves and cleaned up the place
I hear Bob Hall say "It's good to see that homely face"

*So if you are bored and things seem helter skelter
Just spend Saturday night in 'The Old Bombshelter'*

*I beg your pardon, Wayne, I didn't forget you
We know the customers are glad they met you
As for your institution I haven't much more to say
But rest assured we'll be around come next payday.*

The Bombshelter and Horn's Hardware burnt down in the late 1950s. Neighbor, Ruth Miller, remembers that night well, as she lived next door. Her two younger daughters, Kathy and Mary, and the dog were sent across the street to the Burgett home. The fire was so hot that the Fire Department had her stand outside and spray down the side of her house. Curly Burgett used her phone to call dispatch to send more fire trucks from neighboring towns. There was no 911 back in those days. In the wee hours of the night, after the fire was extinguished, Ruth couldn't go back to sleep so she decided to stay up and can the beets that she had planned to process the next day. Dick Porter reports that the sky was blue from the burning alcohol. Becky Moyer Darr remembers serving food to the firefighters.

In the mid 1950s, the Lakeville Inn, site of the first restaurant in town, originally owned by Glen Nizely, was owned by Paul and Hazel Kelly. They added liquor, an 'old time band' of piano, banjo, sometimes a guitar, bones and sometimes spoons, fiddle, washboard, and a wash-tub string base. Becky Moyer Darr shared "As a little 5 year old, I thought they were pretty awesome. Potato chips, pop, and old men making music. What more could a bored little kid ask for?"

Paul Kelly – owner of Kelly's Lakeville Inn – *photo courtesy of Becky Moyer Darr*

"The Band" at Kelly's Lakeville Inn

Current picture of Lakeville Inn, first restaurant.

Future owners of the business were Doyle and Jean Miller, and Terry Jones. Jones operated it as a recycled paper collection site for a while. It is presently a residence.

Pen from Kelly's Lakeville Inn– *photo courtesy of Carl Tope.*

Ken Bauer shared a memory of The Fur House. In the early 1950s it was located on the inside of Horseshoe Alley in the first barn, owned by Howard 'Bony' Rhamey. The second barn was owned by Jim Rhamey. Howard Rhamey and Ken's father, Charles 'Bunny' Bauer, conducted the fur business. Ken remembers one occasion where he had trapped at least 20 muskrats and was pulling them out of his jacket pockets one after another. All his traps were full that day.

We also found the following businesses in Lakeville School yearbooks:

1931 -   L. R. Burgett – local and long distance moving. General hauling

1946 –   Joe Etzwiler Garage

Round Lake Airport – Flying Service, Flight Instruction, Charter Trips, Passenger Flights, Anytime, Anywhere, Visitors Welcome

1948 –   Murphy's Grocery

J. A. Shane – feed

1950 –   Peoples Life Insurance – Ralph Hudson

1951 –   Hitchcock's Welding Shop

1960 –   Jones Market

Troy McIntire – small motor repair

Robert "Curly" Burgett – trucking (dump)

1962 -   LC Metcalf Insurance

Bar-Mar Beauty Salon – owners were Barbara Boals and Martha Schnittke and was located on the east end of the post office building. Barb later conducted her business in her home on Depot Street.

THE LATE 1900s TO PRESENT

In the early 1960s, Bud and Jean Sponseller purchased the business. My sisters and I have many memories of going to Bud's while growing up. A quarter would buy a bottle of pop and a bag of potato chips. Many comic books were purchased there. And, when camping out in the 'back lot', owned by Kenny and Florence Rush, a stop at Bud's for a bag full of penny candy (really a penny at that time) was always a must do. It was a special treat when the family went up, sat in a booth, and had ice cream sundaes or floats.

Jean and Bud Sponseller

The Sponsellers retired in the mid 1970s and sold the business to Ed and Shirley Roberts. Other owners after that were the Lifers, Paul Arnholt, Lee and John Grisetti, Terry Jones, Art Watson, and Diane Cayhill. Diane was the last to run it as a business and then moved the business to the former Woodland Inn near Big Prairie. It is currently a residence.

BUD'S RESTAURANT

In the 1970s, Ben Knox opened up Hilltop Rubber on the west end of the town, next to Lakeville Speedway. They manufactured the rubber middles of golf balls. Today, it is owned by Chris Sparr and houses C&J Performance and Sparrs Axle Machine.

H & H Manufacturing was located four buildings to the east of the school house. It was first operated by Noble Hitchcock and his father, Delbert Hitchcock. It was also known as Hitchcock Welding at some point. The Hitchcocks had a patent for manufacturing front grills for Ford tractors. They also made a tilt model grill for Satoh Japanese tractors. Linda (Burgett) McCullough recalls that Delbert always kept Hershey bars hidden in his desk.

In 1972, Delbert passed away and his widow sold the business to Chris Cagle and Jerry Snyder. Chris managed the manufacturing side and Jerry the sales. They manufactured bumpers and tractor weights. In 1974, they developed the Bale King wagon.

The operation moved to Big Prairie at some point. Later on, when the business split, Bale King and Jerry Snyder stayed in Big Prairie. Jerry later sold out to United Farm Tool and went on to start a Hot Shot Trailer business.

Cagle Manufacturing built sprayers in the Lakeville building. They were in business for around 20 years.

Some of the workers over the years included Richard Welch (H&H), Richard Porter (H&H) and he helped with the move to Big Prairie. Ron (Buckshot) Burgett and Bob Burgett worked in Big Prairie. Mary Ann Taylor Burgett and Chuck Paullin drove truck for them. Mary Tipton worked in the Cagle Manufacturing office.

Another past familiar sight in Lakeville were the Paullin Milk Trucks. John Paullin and his son, Chuck, drove for their family business for many years. They hauled milk 365 days a year, through all kinds of weather, including the blizzard in 1978.

PAULLIN MILK CARTAGE INC.

JOHN PAULLIN
CHUCK PAULLIN

Phone: 827-2063
Lakeville, Ohio

Hamlin Racing Engines is currently located at the former Horn Hardware site next to the railroad crossing. It is owned by Ron Hamlin.

BAUER BOAT SALES

In 1966 Charles Bauer, better known as Bunny Bauer, started a fishing supply and boat business out of his home and farm. He sold live bait, artificial tackle, rods, reels, and anything else fishing/ boating. He also sold boats including Crest and Sanpan Pontoons. Other boats were also sold including Crestliner and Seahawk boats. They sold Johnson outboard engines. Ken Bauer, Bunny's son, worked there on the engines in the service department part time. Ken then took over the operation in 1970 when he returned from the armed services.

In January 1979 the business was sold to Bob Sadler and Les Miller and remained in operation for approximately 13 years at which time the business was moved north of Shreve Ohio. Les Miller bought out the business from Bob two years after the purchase in 1979.

BAUERS CAMP GROUND

On the east side of Lakeville down by the tracks there is a camp ground that has been present since at least 1960. It is currently owned by Ken Bauer but was originally started by his father, Charles (Bunny) Bauer, who owned Bauer Boat sales. Their business was located a mile or so east of Lakeville on State Route 226. Ken stated that he remembers mowing the grass down at the campground when he was a teenager back in 1958 or 1959. Ken stated that his dad started renting the campsites a few at a time. They now have 54 sites. If you look closely from State Route 226 or if you are on the south side of O'Dell's Lake and look across to the campground you may notice a peculiar camper. Well, that is no camper, it's a red caboose. I can only imagine how cool it is inside and how fun it would be to sleep in it. Ken stated that it has been there for at least 30 years.

I was able to speak to Fred, the current owner. He purchased the caboose off of John Kirkendall. The original owner was Don Fulmer who purchased the 1929 model from the railroad. At one point it was used by the Republican Party for their campaigns, pulling it in parades around Ashland County, Ohio.

Fred was nice enough to allow my sisters and me to tour the caboose. This was quite a treat for us as it appears that the original machinery and wood work are all preserved. It still has the charm and character a caboose should have. Now days trains no longer have cabooses which is my favorite part of a train. It's so sad that our children don't get to see them in use rumbling down the tracks.

CUTTIN' IT UP WITH A TOUCH OF SASS

The east side of the Post Office building has been home to beauty salons off and on for many years. It is currently occupied by Cuttin' It Up With A Touch of Sass which is owned by Amy Spreng. She offers services for men, women, and children.

ROUND LAKE GOLF COURSE

Round Lake Golf Course is located on State Route 179, just north of the Route 3 intersection. It sits on 25 beautiful acres. The golf course has been established since around 1928. The greens are bent grass and the fairway grass is winter rye. The course measures 3265 yards from the longest tees. There are two sets of tees for different skill levels where you can play nine holes of golf. Just recently footgolf was introduced.

Back in the 1960 and 1970s the golf course also had a cement inground pool. Many children from the neighborhood rode their bikes out to it to learn how to swim. I believe the pool is history, but you can still play golf, receive lessons and purchase equipment. The course was recently purchased by the Round Lake Christian Camp. From what I have read great things are going to continue to happen with the business.

ROUND LAKE CHRISTIAN CAMP

Round Lake Christian Camp is nestled around Round lake (another kettle lake). It was founded in 1950. It is located on the north side of State Route 3 going east from the Route 179 intersection. The assembly has been in operation for some 39 years. They provide dormitory style housing with bunkbeds and can handle groups of 30 to 400. The Round Lake Christian Camp is a wonderful place to meet and celebrate God.

COUNTRY CORNERS / IRON PONY SALOON

Another long-time establishment is located at the northeast corner of the Route 3 and Route 179 intersection – The Iron Pony Saloon. I know it was Country Corner in the 1970s. It also had several names and owners in between then and now.

COZY CORNERS GAS STATION

On the southwest corner of the same intersection, State Routes 3 and 179, is the former site of Cozy Corners gas station. It is now an empty lot.

WASHINGTON MUTUAL INSURANCE ASSOCIATION

The business with the track record for longevity in Lakeville is Washington Mutual Insurance Association. It was founded in 1878 and is still in business today, as an afiliate of Wayne Mutual Insurance. The following is an excerpt from an article written in 1985 for the book *Holmes County Ohio to 1985*.

In the summer of 1878, ten men of this community, under the leadership of Jacob Schmidt and E. J. Lozier, banded themselves together for mutual protection against the fury of fire and lightning. As in all undertakings of this kind, their trials were many. Their reward from a financial standpoint may not have paid for the effort, but the fact that they were building for posterity, was an incentive they could not ignore. Many meetings were held, and a lot of midnight oil was burned. After many weeks spent in planning and laying a solid foundation, an organization was perfected. On September 18th, 1878, the Secretary of State granted them a charter, On October 22nd, of the same year, the Washington Township Mutual Fire & Lightning Insurance Association began to function.

In 1921 a house and land were purchased on County Road 100 south of Lakeville for the use of the secretary and his office. In 1925 the office was built. This was used by secretaries J. H. Doty and twenty-eight years by Forest Campbell, assisted by his wife, Esther, until retirement in 1973. They were followed by Donald Long, secretary, assisted by Lois Pringle and Patricia Walters.

A larger office was built and moved into January 1977 with the home and other office being sold.

The name was legally changed to Washington Mutual Insurance Association in 1963. This is the only known insurance company to have originated in Holmes County, and the only insurance company with its home office in the county today (1985, the time of this article)

In 2009, an affiliation agreement was signed with Wayne Mutual Insurance Company in Wooster, Ohio. This agreement authorized the existing Wayne Mutual board of directors and company officers to lead both companies. The two companies now work closely together, but operate as separate entities. The office is no longer located at Lakeville.

13

Lakeville Speedway

Lakeville, the sleepy little town nestled at the west end of O'Dell's Lake, did not look like a popular place to be on a Friday or Saturday night, but it was, due to the popularity of Lakeville Speedway set high on a hill on State Route 226 outside of the town. The racetrack was opened in 1964 by owners Harry (Nick) Wigton and Wade Puster. The track was a 3/8 mile clay oval with semi banked turns. The speedway was one of the most challenging places to race because of the clay used, and it had a specific amount of dirt on the track and the length of track being smaller. Lakeville was one of the first local tracks to offer mini sprint car racing.

Al McCurdy, a later owner, would spend hours making sure the track was maintained properly for driver safety. EMT and ambulances were present in the center of the track during every race, ready to go in case of a crash with injuries. One time the EMT themselves needed an ambulance. A certain EMT's husband jumped into the driver's side and drove off before the EMT was completely in the unit and came tumbling out the back of the ambulance. I remember seeing this because I was sitting in the stands that night.

Some of top drivers in the 1970's were Jim Gentry and Dean Alexander who drove "hardtop" cars, while Jac Haudenschild and Kenny Jacobs were featured in the sprint cars. They both later advanced to the World of Outlaws Series. Jac won his first race at Lakeville Speedway when he was 15 years old. Jac is still racing today at Wayne County Speedway and all over the United States with the All Star Circuit of Champions, finishing in 9th place in 2018. Both Jacobs and Haudenschild have been inducted into the National Sprint Car Hall of Fame, Jacobs in 2007 and Haudenschild in 2009.

Another great, the late NASCAR driver, Tim Richmond, ran some practice laps there while he was a crew chief. It was his first time in a race car and was reported to have had faster laps than his driver.

I will admit that my favorite driver was Jim Gentry in good old car #14, I loved his battles on the track against Dean Alexander. Those were the best of times at the Speedway!

The track had become an icon to the area and surrounding counties, with large crowds coming every weekend and the roar of the engines could be plainly heard in the town. I remember being able to see the rise of the dust, the gleaming lights and hear the sound of the cars racing around the track from the back playground behind the school where we would stand watching in the direction of the track when we did not have permission to go to the races on a particular night.

Many local guys would build their own "Hoopies"; versions of stripped down vehicles that they would use as "push trucks". My sister particularly remembers Eddie Traxler having his own "Hoopie', other "Hoopie" drivers were Lloyd Wirt, Bob White from Springville.

Current aerial view of Lakeville Speedway. It is owned by an Amish family; however, the EPA won't allow them to put in a pond or to farm it due to the oil and fuel in the soil.

14

LAKEVILLE AND THE 1969 JULY 4th FLOOD

Certain events you never forget regardless of your age. I was only 6 years old on July 4th 1969. Like it happened yesterday, I remember my mother bringing all of us children down to the living room to sleep. I watched the constant strikes of lightning illuminating the etched clipper ship windows with an eerie glow. I don't know if I slept much that night as my mother paced, worried about Dad out on rescue missions with the fire department. There was no TV, no lights, no noise except the pounding of the rain and clapping of thunder.

It was Friday July 3rd 1969. It is reported that the rain started sometime after 9:30pm, halting further celebration of the 4th of July. All the night time festivities were cancelled as people began running to their vehicles, out of the pouring rain. Some reported that it rained so hard they had to stop their vehicles frequently because they were unable to see the road. It rained for approximately 8 hours straight.

The rain totals differ but it is stated that there was between 7 to 18 inches of rain that fell in Holmes and Wayne Counties. The '69 flood is recorded to be the 2nd worst flood in history for Holmes County and is listed as the worst natural disaster.

Holmes County officials had little information about what was going on in Lakeville as the village was cut off from them due to all the flooding and they were busy with the devastation in the Killbuck area. Being a close-knit community meant that a lot of times you had to handle situations on your own. Our fire department did just that.

Photos on this page contributed by Diane Ling. Taken by her father, Kenny Ling.

Ken Bauer remembers all the corn cobs floating down Lake O'Dell from the flooded Equity. I remember standing at the top of the hill looking down across the tracks seeing all the flooding. The Lakeville Booster Club Park was also flooded.

Photo taken by Kenny Ling.

There was one rescue that I remember well that involved a childhood friend, Cindy Tope Bernard. According to Ruth Miller, (Cindy's grandmother who slept through the whole storm), she dropped Cindy off at her son-in-laws (John McCune) who lived in a mobile home on County Rd 100 for the night after spending the evening at West Holmes to watch the fireworks. Ruth had to work in the morning. Ruth stated that she tried to go to Loudonville to work but was stopped by the police at the corner of State Routes 179 and 3. He told Ruth "You're not going anywhere today, lady. It's all flooded". Ruth turned her car around and went back home. Cindy Tope Bernard remembers the night of the flood and has submitted the following story:

I was 6 years old July 4th 1969. At age 6 I don't think your sense of danger is apparent. Looking back, I am sure thankful. I went to the fireworks with my Grandma, Ruth Miller. Afterwards she took me to my cousin Johnny McCune and my Uncle John's mobile home on County Road 100, Lakeville, as she had to work the next morning. I remember it was late and dark and I just wanted to go home. I believe we got popcorn when I got there to brighten me up. I cannot recall if it was raining then or if it started after we went to sleep.

Next thing I know is my Uncle is telling Johnny and me to get up. When I put my foot to the floor I remember stepping in water and thinking I stepped in a bucket of water and why was it by my bed. I remember Johnny saying he thought he was dreaming that he was swimming. My Uncle took us into the kitchen and sat us up on the counter tops as water was rising. I have no idea how high it was at that time but am assuming was rising quickly. He took the curtains down from the kitchen windows and wrapped them around us and I do remember I was shivering and we were all wet. Uncle John did open the door a few times and was looking up the road to see if the firetrucks were coming to get us. I think they were down at the bridge by the Lakeville Equity and could not get through our road.

I think I most likely became afraid when the trailer seemed to be swaying and the dishes were falling out of the cupboard. I really do not know the time span of any of this but I believe it was early morning when the neighbors (Marmets) who lived on the corner of CR 100 and State Route 179 came to us in a rowboat and got us out and took us up to their home. I kind of remember being in the boat but can't remember the process of getting into it and getting to the house. I do remember they gave us hot chocolate and that was very cool.

I can only imagine what my uncle must have been going through as he had 2 small children and was stranded in the flood along with knowing he was losing his home. John did lose everything as I recall being told but we all survived and after hearing all the tragedies throughout the counties of Holmes, Wayne, Ashland, and Coshocton. I know Killbuck was probably the worst hit. I know we were blessed. I remember listening to a radio show many years ago maybe it was 2009 (would have been 40 years) and many stories were told about folks involved, people who lost their lives, and many family tragedies. It really seems so surreal now as I was so young but it was a major catastrophe for our area.

We actually found one of my cousin's stuffed animals one time while walking along the rail road tracks as my friends and I often did. I don't remember how many years later that would have been but a few I imagine. It was a sad feeling.

It is ironic that to this day I am a true water lover. I love to swim, boat, go to the beach and lakes and just be near water. I am thankful for the neighbors and those who were concerned and helped to get us rescued and that we were all safe and I have no trauma or fear of water from the experience.

Dick Porter stated he was around 13-14 years old at the time of the flood and was a witness to the rescue of Cindy and the McCunes. He stated that Chuck Porter, his father, was trying to rescue them with his John Deere "A" tractor. Because the tractor had no lights, they shined the firetruck's spotlights on the scene. There were questions if the tractor was heavy enough to withstand the current but the rescue was attempted. Chuck thought he was driving on the road, but, either the water washed the tractor off the road or he drove off the berm. John Rush was standing on the back of the tractor and jumped off at that time. Then Chuck fell off the tractor into the floodwater and started to get swept away. He managed to grab ahold of something to stop him. John then threw a rope to Chuck. When Dick saw his father in danger he ran out to John in the floodwater and grabbed ahold of the rope to help his dad to safety. The rest of the firemen joined in. Eventually, Nashville Fire Department arrived with a boat and rescued the group from the mobile home. Cindy and the McCunes were taken to the safety of the Marmet home.

The John Deere survived but had to be rebuilt. Chuck Porter received a plaque from the fire department for his efforts in the rescue. Cindy and Johnny got candy from Buds in the morning and the siding of the mobile home is now on Ruth's garage.

Dick Porter also reported that a man drove over the railroad tracks down at the Lakeville Booster Club Park and went into the water. He was swept away when he got out of the car but managed to grab ahold of a tree until he was rescued by Nashville Fire Department.

Chuck Porter's Service Plaque from the Fire Department –*Photo courtesy of Dick Porter*

Flood pictures on this page taken by Kenny Ling, submitted by Diane Ling

Picture to right was taken looking west from railroad crossing at the park.

The truck driver hauling this heavy equipment over the bridge, left his cab door open just in case the bridge at Lakeville Booster Club Park collapsed.

Lakeville Booster Club Park under water during 1969 July Flood- *Photo taken by Kenny Ling*

Photo by Pat Walters

Photos on this page were taken by Pat Walters. The top picture is a bulldozer that was brought in to work on the railroad tracks. Underneath it is a close up of a bulldozer that got stuck. Also shown is a photo of the Lakeville Equity.

Above is the grassy area between the Booster Club Park pavilion and the railroad tracks. Note the outhouse in the corner. To the left is a picture of washed out railroad ties.

15

The Great Blizzard of 1978

The Blizzard of 1978 would rate near or at the top of the list of natural disasters for the Holmes County and Wayne County area. The storm has often been referred to as the "White Hurricane" bringing extreme winter conditions of snowfall and high winds.

Here are the scientific facts of the storm:

The storm struck Wednesday, January 25 and raged through Friday, January 27, 1978. Snow fell and high winds followed, forming huge snowdrifts, some reported as tall as twenty feet high. Cars were completely buried in drifts and people were stuck in their homes without electricity and heat for a few days. Kids were happy to get out of going to school for those days. I know I was thrilled to stay in bed in the mornings. We were lucky at my home because we had a natural gas furnace, so we stayed warm.

The snowstorm was a historic blizzard that struck the Ohio Valley and Great Lakes Region. Winds gusting up to 100 miles per hour caused drifts that nearly buried some homes and cars. Seventy total storm-related deaths are contributed to this storm with fifty-one of the seventy occurring in Ohio.

Ohio National Guardsmen were called in to rescue people and many local people and police departments used snowmobiles and four-wheel drive vehicles to move rescued people with no heat. Many people went to stay with friends and neighbors, while rescue personnel took food to stranded families and their animals.

Looking down TR 1060 – *photo courtesy of Lisa Ferris Miller*

Looking East on County Road 100 and TR511 – *photo courtesy of Lisa Ferris Miller*

My sister, Shelly, and her fiancé, Larry Spade, recalled walking from Lakeville to our parent's new property on County Road 100 to check on the house while it was still in its building stage. She said that they were walking on top of snow drifts that were over five feet deep.

Some other memories from the storm: Linda Burgett McCullough recalls that her father, Curly Burgett, was a Washington Township trustee at the time and performed the plowing. Deb Shriver Smith's father delivered the mail for neighboring Big Prairie. He broke his back while trying to put mail into a box that had ice under the snow. That put an end to his mail carrying career. Don and Barb Long lived on County Road 100 and she remembers how the strength of the winds made their house shudder.

Many Lakeville area residents opened up their homes to neighbors and families with no heat. Fire Department volunteers went to homes and farms to check on families, bringing water, groceries, and medications if needed.

The Lakeville Fire Department and local volunteers worked tirelessly to serve their community and played a crucial part in restoring electrical power to the area. The Ohio Power Company had no access to get to their substation on State Route 754 to restore power without someone clearing the path. Since Washington Township had the largest snow mover with a huge "V" shape plow in the area, the Township Trustees met with Lakeville Fire Department and Ron Kick, who plowed for the township, to plan a way to get power restored.

Their adventure started out with the snow mover or better known as "The Maintainer", plowing a route along State Route 226 to Shreve Fire Department to pick up the Ohio Power workers then moving down State Routes 514 and 754, only to be stopped by drifts about a mile away from the substation. They had to radio the Lakeville and Shreve Fire Departments in order to bring out four-wheel drive vehicles loaded with snowmobiles. The workers were able to reach the switches at the substation, restoring power to areas north of State Route 39, but the areas south of State Route 39 could not be restored due to damaged or downed lines. The group traveled back to Shreve, then to Lakeville, making their way along State Route 179 to the other substation located there. Once repairs were made, the group continued back to Shreve and back down to the substation off State Route 754 to switch the power back on. The procession consisted of sixteen vehicles, the Maintainer, four-wheel drive vehicles, a bulldozer, Ohio Power trucks, snowplows, and snowmobiles. All they needed was a marching band to complete the parade!

24" of snow on top of trash can lid–
photo courtesy of Lisa Ferris Miller

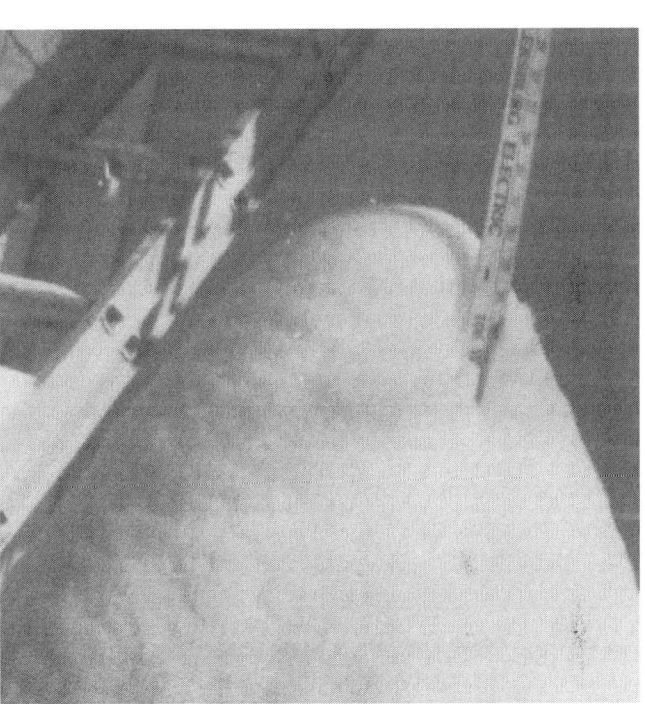

Ronnie "Buckshot" Burgett

County Road 100 before and after plowing – *photos courtesy of Lisa Ferris Miller*

16

Lakeville Schools

Over the years, Lakeville had 3 schools, located at different sites.

The Original School Building

The original one-room building, known as Number 7, was located at the present intersection of Routes 179/226 and Route 3. This area was known as Colliers Crossing. This was also the original location of the town of Lakeville. The one-room school building was moved in the 1870s to the second hill towards the present site of Lakeville. According to the 1978 Holmes County Antique Festival Book, that building was still being used as a home in 1978. When moved, it was located in a field on the south side of Donald and Kathryn (Teenie) Mackey's driveway. It was moved again in the early 1930s to its present location at the far end of the driveway. Mrs. Mackey's grandparents, Charles and Ellen Wachtel, lived in the house at that time. The Don Mackey family lived there for a while, and then moved next door into the home of her parents, Mark and Olive Miller, where they continue to live today.

Lakeville Yesterday and Today

The current owners of the old schoolhouse are Barbara and Terry Sparr. They have lived there for over 40 years. The building would not be recognized as it has been extensively remodeled and a second floor has been added. The top and bottom of the picture on the previous page shows the front and back view of Number 7. The middle picture is of the current school building, as it looked in 1925. The picture is from the 1925 yearbook, The Trial. The picture to the right shows the building today. The roofline on the right-hand lower level is the original roofline. An addition was added on the first floor to the left-hand side and the second floor was also added. This home is located at the end of a long private lane. We request that you respect their privacy and do not drive back to see it.

Brick Two-Room School

A brick, two-room school replaced the original building in 1882. It was constructed somewhere in the area between the baseball field and the race track. It was later torn down when the current building was built in 1914. Not much more could be found about this building.

Shown below is a 1911 School Souvenir.

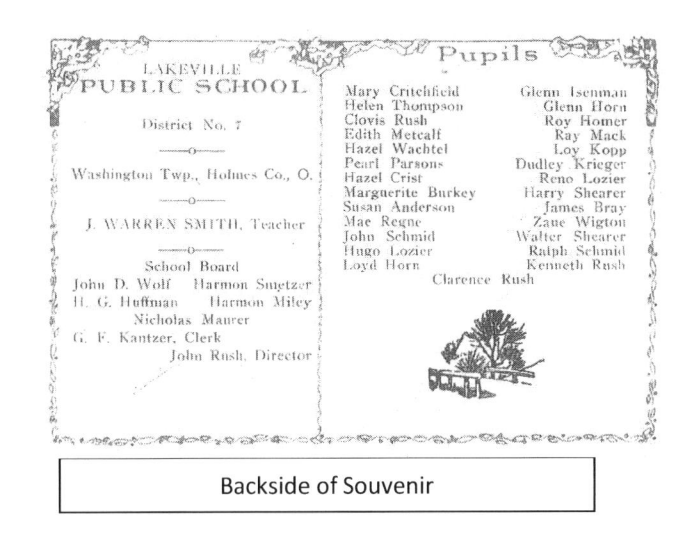

Front of Souvenir

Backside of Souvenir

The Current Lakeville Special School

Above the southwest door of the current school building there is a large cast cement plaque with letters nine inches tall declaring that the structure is "Lakeville Special School." One may wonder, what exactly makes that school special?

The following facts were gathered from two newspaper articles, "Lakeville Knows Its School Is Special" written by James S Orchard, Lakeville principal, published in the Daily Record in 1984, and a second article, "Progressive Education in 1913" written by Ed DeGraw, published in the Times Reporter on February 29, 1984.

In 1972, John Phillips compiled a record of old school board minutes dating from April 1913 thru April 1914. On April 1, 1913, a group of Lakeville and vicinity citizens met at the Lakeville School house to discuss plans for a better educational facility.

Participating in the meeting were Albert Butler, Scott Lozier, David Collier, John Horn, Jacob Miller, Phillip Sharr, and George Eseman. Butler was named as Chairman of the group and Scott Lozier was appointed as Secretary.

A committee of three was selected to go to the Board of Education of Washington Township and request that a second-grade township high school be built in Lakeville during the summer and be ready for school to open on September 1, 1913.

These men were ahead of their time and were about to request a plan that had never been incorporated in area education. Not only were they asking for a three-year high school for Lakeville, but they also wanted special boundaries for the district that would cross county lines.

Construction of current building - 1914

Collier made a motion that *"We either incorporated, or petition for a special district unless the Board of Education of Washington Township grants us better facilities for education."* The motion was approved.

The committee sent the petition to the township school board and received a counter proposal. That proposal did not meet with the village citizens' approval. They voted to disregard it and went about putting together a school district of their own – a "special" district. The new district would include areas in both Wayne and Ashland counties, which was unheard of at the time; however, they felt that better education should not be bound by county lines. They wanted to share their new facility with their friends and neighbors in the adjoining counties.

On May 27, 1913, Probate Judge R. W. Taneyhill accepted the committee's petition and granted into law the designation of Lakeville Special School District.

The Lakeville Special School District Board of Education was established on July 12, 1913. Albert Butler was elected president; Scott Lozier, vice president; S. P. Kopp, clerk, and Jacob Miller, treasurer.

The first superintendent / teacher, S.S. Simpson, was hired at $80 per month. Principal, Gladys Huffman received $60 per month. Teachers received $50 per month and janitors, $40.

Sealed bids were submitted for the job of transporting students from the "south district." John Wigton won the bid at $2.50 a day for a long route and $2 for a short route. Mrs. J.M. Graven, a teacher, received $7 a month extra to bring her students to school. A horse stable was to be furnished by the board of education.

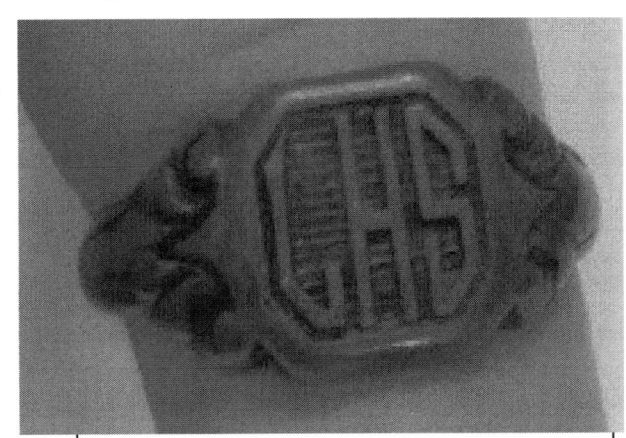

Lakeville High School class ring that belonged to Vera Butler – *photo courtesy of Bob Walters*

By March of 1914, it was decided that G.C. Butler was to build the new school building and assembly hall for $11,272. The name "Lakeville Special School" was to be inscribed on the entrance lintel.

In its early days, Lakeville Special School taught all 12 grades. 1918 saw the building's first graduating class of 4 students. The 1931 yearbook, Oak Leaves, alumni news lists the graduates as Bessie Rush, Kenneth Rush, Edith Graven, and Hazel Harriss.

Additions to the building were made in the 1930s, 1986, and 1997. The following excerpt from the 1931 year book, Oak Leaves, talks about the 1931 addition:

Vera Butler's light blue Lakeville High School Class of 1926 tassel -*photo courtesy of Bob Walters*

Our New School

With the opening of school in 1931, a new period in the history of Lakeville Special School begins. At last the boys and girls of Lakeville district will be given the opportunities which other children in the county have already had. No longer need we make excuses for our school. Lakeville will stand among the first in educational equipment and facilities. The school is the center of much of the social life of the community, and its welfare therefore concerns everyone. That this is true has been demonstrated by the fine support given by the voters.

The following class pictures are from the 1925 year book, The Trial.

Mechanical Drawing, Lakeville

Scoring Dairy Cow, Lakeville

Shop Work, Lakeville.

One of the additions in the 1930s required the demolition of the Plimpton Guard Armory, located on the east side of the school. Prior to its destruction, the school had used it for boys' basketball games and class plays.

1946 Staff – Front row, from left: Mrs. Franks, Mrs. Rhamey, and Mrs. Dilgard.

Second row: Mr. Franks, Mrs. Gindlesberger, and Miss Lepley

1946 - 7th and 8th Grade

Front row, from left, Clarence Lemon, Kathryn Lemon, Lucille McKinley, Leo Tope, Harold Wachtel, Dean Acker.
Second row, Mrs. Rhamey, Jimmy Flinner, Paul Kiner, Charlene Anderson, Barbara Shriver, Wade Gindlesberger, Richard Crawford.
Third Row, Roger Albertson, Marilyn Horner, Patsy Scott.

Absent---------------Robert Johnson, Natalie Greegor.

New Student--------------------------Patty Vicars

1953 – The Sentinel Year Book - Bus Drivers – Howard Rhamey and Floyd Ferris

1953 - Custodian - Carl (Dave) Wigton

Avis Ireland
Margaret Crawford
Edna McIntire
Dorothy Rhamey

1953 - Cafeteria Cooks

110

1953 *Fourth & Fifth Grades* LAKEVILLE

First Row: Norma Jean Miller, Nancy Akins, Patty Buren, Sharon Weber, Margaret Ferris, Sharon Snyder, Betty Shisler
Second Row: Geneva Fortney, Thomas Horn, Charles Puster, Thomas Rhamey, David Miller, Rexford Rickly, Joe Etzwiler
Third Row: Robert Wagner, Alyce Chipner, Robert Gwin, Mary Ann Miller, Donald Ferris, Mrs. Lillian Sprang
Fourth Row: Ronald Mosher, Hazel Robinson, Wanda Robinson, Lois Kay Horn, Kenneth Bauer

Around 1952, the state of Ohio revoked Lakeville's charter. In 1953, high school students from Lakeville were able to go to other high schools in the area. That same year, Big Prairie and Lakeville consolidated. Grades one through four stayed at both Big Prairie and Lakeville. Grades 5, 6, 7, and 8 all went to Lakeville, and grades 9 through 12 went to Big Prairie for high school.

1955 The Sentinel Year Book Picture

FIRST AND SECOND GRADE — LAKEVILLE

First Grade—Susie Etzwiler, Linda Lou Wigton, Billy Wagner, Linda Lee Buswell, Sandra Sigler, Dean Miller, Loretta Tate, Connie Vicars, Peggy Ferris.

Second Row—Eddie Lozier, Ruth Ann Breitenbucher, Larry Miller, Eddie Arnold, Sandy Burgett, Bobby Burgett, Karen Crawford.

Third Row—Shirley Ferris, Jacquie Gilliam, Linda Lozier, Sue Ann Doty, Kenneth Stake, Garneta Aber, Mrs. Franks.

1957 The Sentinel Year Book Pictures

FRESHMEN

First Row—Clark Sprang, Dale McIntire, Kenneth Justice, Bob Wagner, Donald Franks, Roger Gwin.

Second Row—Marilyn Franks, Terry Jones, Danny Garver, Jim Jones, Pat Fleming, Virginia Spreng, Sandra Neiswander, Judy McClure.

Third Row—Mr. Nagy, Patrica O'Neil, Loretta Justice, Danny Breitenbucher, Glen Cassidy, Judy Matheny, Marilyn Cornell, Mary Ann Miller.

Fourth Row—Kenny Bauer, Danny Dye, Roger Conner, Nelson Lozier, Jay McIntire, Bob Kauffman, Donald Ferris.

President—Pat Fleming; Vice President—Jim Jones; Secretary—Danny Garver; Treasurer—Virginia Spreng; Student Council—Terry Jones, Sandra Neiswander.

RESERVES

First Row—Kenny Bauer, John Boals, Glen Cassidy, Danny Dye, Harold Bigler, Coach Robert Lee.

Second Row—Forest Tate, Jack Johnson, Dick Anderson, Jerry Hendershott, Nelson Lozier, Jim Jones, Donnie Franks.

GRADES ONE AND TWO—LAKEVILLE

First Row—Jane Schnittke, Peggy Shearer, Ronald Vicars, Bobby Taylor, Cheryl Jeffries, Elaine Spreng, Carol Mosher, Wesley Tate, John Lozier, Penny Paullin.

Second Row—Harrison Murphy, Olin Olney, Sandra Hulderman, Rodger Lozier, Larry Lorentz, Nancy Thompson, James Boals, Diana Trapp, Charles Bauer.

1962 The Sentinel Year Book pictures

First and Second Grade (Lakeville)

ROW 1, L to R: Terry Miller, Rosa Lee Marmet, Beulah Bookman, Randy Sponseller, Steven Ferris, Rexanne Long, John Kick.
ROW 2, L to R: Francis Trapp, Deborah Paullin, Gwen Bailey, Lewis Beech, Kim Ogg, Kip Ogg, Teresa Bailey.
ROW 3, L to R: Christine Mosher, Virginia Wigton, Lester Wise, Ricky Aylsworth, Connie Sellers, Linda Freeman.
ROW 4, L to R: Katherine Lemon, Michael Butler, Linda Burgett, Daryl Woodruff, Sharon Lozier.

Third and Fourth Grade (Lakeville)

ROW 1, L to R: John Mosher, Berniece Tate, Dick Porter, Roger Spanseller, Kathy Miller, Jane Paullin, Linda Parks.
ROW 2, L to R: Dianna Jefferies, Jim Mosher, Tim Hitchock, Marilyn Miller, Elaine Knox, Barbara Wise.
ROW 3, L to R: Kathy Beech, Carol Lorentz, Debbie Bailety, Tom De Weese, Linda Wise, Phyllis Trapp, Mrs. Taillon.
ROW 4, L to R: Becky Herbert, Ann Wachtel, Richard Ferris, Don Taylor, Loretta Austin, Catherine Derr.

Fifth and Sixth Grades (Lakeville)

ROW 1, L to R: Janice Parks, Linda Franks, Colleen O'Donnell, Mary Ferris, Robert Tompson, Randall Ross, Richard Woodruff, Geraldine Spreng.
ROW 2, L to R: Dick Taylor, Douglas Dye, Patricia Murphy, Jane Miller, Jack Tipton, Bradley Fath, Mr. Moore.
ROW 3, L to R: Jim Leadbetter, Floyd Robinson, John Lozier, Robert Taylor, Ronnie Vickers.
ROW 4, L to R: Karen Snoddy, Cheryl Jeffries, Peggy Bowen, Kathy Crawford, Penny Paullin, David Basquin.

1963 The Sentinel Yearbook Picture

First and Second Grade (Lakeville)

ROW 1: L to R: Sandra Albertson, Cathy Freeman, Karen Knox, Patty Aylsworth, Susie Taylor, Lawrene Spade, Kenny Jones, Jerry Parks, Ricky Fortune.
ROW 2: L to R: Kay Wigton, Diane Ling, Sue Kick, Gwen Bailey, Debra Paullin, Christine Mosher, Rosa-Lee Marmet, Connie Sellers.
ROW 3: L to R: Beulah Book, Clifford Long, Ronnie Burgett, John Kick, Butch Trapp, Terry Miller.
ROW 4: L to R: Lester Wise, Dan Mosher, Buddy Beech, Randy Sponseller, Steve Ferris, Teacher: Mrs. Waltour.

In 1965, the west end of Holmes County was formed into West Holmes School District. Grades K-6 remained in their current communities, the middle school consolidated into the town of Millersburg, and a new high school was built several miles west of Millersburg.

Later additions to the Lakeville property involved buying the two properties located to the east side, the home of Don and Sandy Wigton, and the land where the former Walter and Odessa Ferris home had been located. The land was turned into a driveway and additional parking

Several locals to grace the halls of Lakeville Special School were Rod and Faye Franks, Erma Gindlesberger, Vera Butler, Ralph Hudson, Elizabeth Rhamey, and Carl (Dave) Wigton.

The Franks lived in the house directly to the east of the school, later owned by the Schnittke's and then the Wigtons. Roderick Franks taught and was Superintendnt at the Lakeville School for many years. His wife, Faye, taught in Holmes County for 50 years, with just over 20 of those in Lakeville.

Erma Gindlesberger, (1901-1995), lived two doors to the east from Vera. She lived in Lakeville for 52 years. She had many roles in her 35 years of teaching in Holmes County. She taught English and Latin and spent eight years at West Holmes High School as a librarian.

Erma Gindlesberger

Vera Butler, (1907-1983), lived across the street from the school. She graduated from Lakeville School and taught at Nashville school for many years. Vera finished her career as a second grade teacher at Nashville Elementary

Ralph Hudson was a long time resident of Lakeville and taught in Ashland and Holmes county for 37 years.

Carl (Dave) Wigton lived on the east end of the town and was a long-time custodian at the school. His picture is from the 1957 Big Prairie – Lakeville yearbook, The Sentinel.

CARL WIGTON

The following pictures were submitted by B B Ferris

Back row—Junior Shearer, Forest Evens, Carl Wigton, John Thompson, Floyd Ferris, Lawrence Smith, Edward Kopp. Second row—Supt. Glasgo, Boyd Ferris, Milo Shaffer, Marvin McClure, Robert Smith, James Parson, Edward Ostrander, Walter Horn, Mr. Yarman. Front row—Julia Zimmerman, Gladys Shearer, Beatrice Renison, Ruth Miller, Mae Gilbert, Doris Shearer, Neva Rush, Wava Fulmer, Miss Williams.

Back row—John Long, Donald Burgett, Glen Johnson, Carl Kopp, Donald McKinley, Harry Wigton, Carl Greathouse. Third row—Miss Skelley, Carrie Tope, Jean Drumm, Betty Krieger, Leona Smith, Violet Hall, Aeolus Rush, Miss Williams, Farrell Wigton. Second row—Opal Taylor, Marjorie Bender, Mary Richey, Ruth Long, Thelma Smith, Virginia Shearer, Beulah Kopp, Dorothy Drake, Louise Horn, Hazel Horner, Geneva Smith. Front row—William Tope, Warren Gilbert, Clell Horner, Walter Ferris, Paul Johnson, Freddie Schoolcraft.

Raymond Snyder, Treas.
Ruth Morris, Pres.
Roger Acker, Sec.
E. H. Youngen, Supt.

Leoma Flickinger

CLASS OF 1942
LAKEVILLE HIGH SCHOOL
LAKEVILLE, OHIO.

PHOTOS BY
LIBERTY STUDIOS
WOOSTER, O.

John Tope Jr.

Homer Cayhoe
Sarah Ashcraft
Betty Carpenter
Harold Jeffries

17

Lakeville United Methodist Church

Religion was an important element early in Lakeville's history. Although there was no church erected, Cornelius Quick organized religious meetings and classes in 1828, congregating in the cabins near Lovett's (Bonnet's) Corner and the original area of the first Lakeville.

In 1883, townspeople had pledges of $1846 for construction of a church. The Lakeville Methodist Church was finally built and was dedicated on March 1, 1885, with Reverend H.A. Smith as the first minister. From 1885 to 1904, Lakeville Methodist Church was on a circuit with Nashville and Newkirk churches with sermons being held every two weeks.

While growing up in Lakeville during the 1960s thru 1980s, the church was an integral part of the community, having fellowship dinners, summer Vacation Bible School, and a community choir made up of local children. People would come from miles around for the annual Turkey Dinner that was held in November before Thanksgiving, which was always sold out. It was immensely popular, giving people a chance to socialize and share a home-style meal with members and friends in the community.

Lakeville Methodist Church has seen many renovations over the years, a major one being the belfry strategically moving from the east side to the west side of the building. Other additions have been added over the years. The church is still active today in the community providing weekly church services and a food pantry.

The Sunday school class headed by Howard Taylor was active in the 1976 Bicentennial Celebration with the class painting an original design decorated with the American eagle. The sign was erected outside the church and was there for many years. Many members of the church sewed their own pioneer outfits for the parade and celebration.

Photo from 1907 Atlas

LAKEVILLE M E. CHURCH

Current pastor – Steve Sullivan

Interior photos taken by Bonnie Porter

Lakeville United Methodist Church
FIX YOUR EYES ON JESUS !
SERVICE SUN 9AM

Current picture of Lakeville United Methodist Church.

121

Celebrating the nation's 200th Anniversary in 1976 in style.

18

Lakeville Post Office

Lakeville Post Office was established on April 4, 1854 and still remains in operation to this day, in a permanent building erected in 1958. Mail was sent by stagecoach to Wooster and then sent to Lakeville every week by carriers on horses, then from Lakeville the mail was carried to Nashville and Glenmont. Post-boys were the earliest carriers of the mail in this area, traveling the Great Trail in Ohio by horseback.

The early post offices in Lakeville were located at the bar in the pool hall area and another post office was located in a building down from the church on the same side of the road. Many early towns had numerous post office locations throughout the years, because the Postmaster job evolved around local politics, so whenever a local government power change occurred usually the result was the current Postmaster being terminated and another one appointed. This is the reason that the early post offices were moved so frequently to different locations, most being operated out of the current Postmaster's home or place of business.

Front view photo of Post Office that was located beside the Lakeville United Methodist Church. – Photo provided by Bob Walters.

Post Office: Lakeville, OH 44638 (Previous Site)

In March of 2000, Postmaster Gary Edwards was quoted in the area newspaper saying that even though Lakeville is a small community it has a large postal demand, with Lakeville Post Office having the largest revenue in Holmes County, sometimes in a single day processing over 100,000 pieces of mail.

Here is a list of all the Postmasters since Lakeville has had an established Post Office.

1. Sullivan Crow
2. Bill Rhamey
3. Jane Davenport
4. Pauline Thompson
5. Ellen Hudson
6. Ralph Shafer
7. Jewel Edwards
8. Gary Edwards
9. James Thompson
10. Oakley Thompson

Post Office as it currently looks

19

LAKEVILLE FIRE DEPARTMENT

Built by love for the community, Lakeville Fire Department had its beginning in 1952 on land donated by brothers Ralph, Lester, and John Hudson. It was a huge project for the Booster Club and the surrounding community. The project broke ground on Labor Day 1952. The building was located beside the Post office and across from Lakeville United Methodist Church. Nearly all the sweat to build the firehouse was provided by the Booster members and friends in the area. Donations were collected including $1,600.00 from Lakeville School. Money was also raised with community events like pie socials and donations from businesses and families in the area.

The original 1952 Lakeville Fire Department building.

The solid block building housed a pumper that could carry 800 gallons of water. With the generous donations and fund raisers, Lakeville had some of the most up to date and state of the art equipment available including plenty of water hoses, 2-way radios and walkie talkies. The Booster club also raised the money for the siren. In the early 70s they also had a red emergency van.

This 1956 Ford fire truck is one of their original vehicles. It is still in operation. The fire department uses it for grass fires because it is lighter and will not get stuck in the fields.

The fire department originated in the minds of 5 men that grew into 33 members. Lakeville Fire Department was one of the first small departments to have a map showing the location of every residence and business within their service area. It was posted on a 4ft x 8ft board and was drawn by Curly Burgett. According to the local news it took 8 hours to be completed. The fire department served Washington Township and the Lakeville School district area.

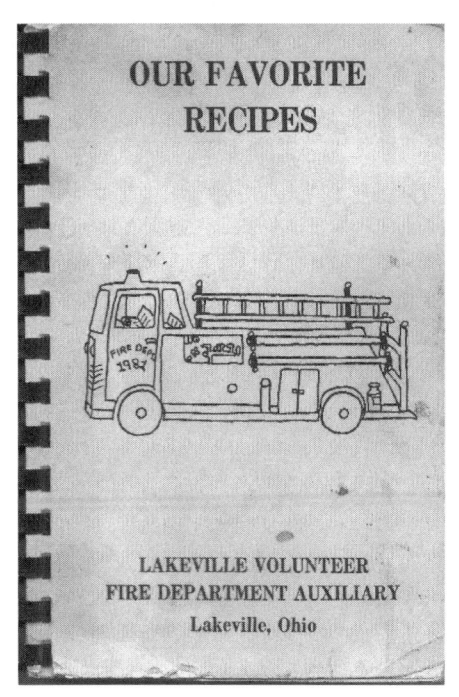

Since approximately 1970, the fire department has been raising money by hosting chicken dinners at Lakeville Elementary school. The popularity of this event has grown over the years. The lines just get longer. They have some great food like homemade noodles, and mashed potatoes. During local fair time the Fire department has a booth and raises money with their mouse trap game. This game has been around since the 1970s and is a favorite game to watch at the local fairs. The smooth operation of the Fire department was also achieved with help from the Ladies Auxiliary Club which was usually the wives of the firemen. They hosted events like the annual Christmas party. During long fire events they would set up food stations and provide drinks and nourishment to the firemen. The women also published a cook book with all the women's favorite recipes. I am sure this book is still in use. I know mine and my sisters' are. They have also hosted a soup and salad supper in March since 1992.

But one of my most favorite memories of the fire department was when Howard Taylor would come back from Lake Erie with a whole cooler of Lake Erie Perch. Oh, the fish fries we had! To this day I have never tasted fish as good. I ate so much fish I would get sick to my stomach. I don't remember the other food items only the fish. I'm sure they were good too. The community always came together and had a great time back in the 70s.

In 1989 the Lakeville Fire Department was taken over by Holmes County. When asked, Don Wigton stated that not many of the firemen were for the takeover but they really had no choice due to the financial situation. The firemen were required to have professional training in order to continue their services. In retrospect the training was beneficial in keeping the firemen safe.

By the 1990s the little firehouse became too small and the community, firemen, and auxiliary came together and raised funds to build a bigger fire station. Ground was broken for the station in January 1992. It is situated east of the old building and is on a 1 ½ acre lot. Many people and local businesses donated time, money and materials once again to safeguard the community. The new building was 44ft x 64ft but had an addition built in 1996. The old firehouse was sold at auction in April 1993.

Western Holmes County Fire District AKA: Lakeville Fire Department members May 9th 2018

Lakeville, along with Nashville Fire department, now service what is called the Western Holmes County Region. Lakeville Fire Department has 35 volunteer members. On average they respond to approximately 7-8 calls a month. Jeff Burgett is the current Chief. Special thanks go out to all the department members past and present who volunteered their time and jeopardized their safety and still do to this day to keep the community safe.

New building constructed in 1992 on the east side of the Post Office.

Newest member of the Lakeville fleet

Robert "Pete" Moyer

Long-time firefighters, Bob Burgett, above, and Don Wigton, left, receiving awards from Lakeville Station and Nashville Station Fire Chiefs Jeff Burgett and Shawn Young.

20

Lakeville Organizations

LAKEVILLE BOOSTER CLUB

Over the years I'm sure there were many clubs and organizations in Lakeville. One of the most beneficial to the community had to be the Lakeville Booster Club. The first meeting was held May 22, 1950 in the school lunch room. Elected officials included: President, Emerson Dilgard; Vice-President, Wade Puster; 2nd Vice-President, Carl Maurer; Secretary, Marjorie Boals; and Treasurer, Olive Miller. Meetings were held the last Monday of each month. Members had to be at least 18 years old and pay yearly dues of $1 per person. The club's purpose was 'to promote any worthy project for the good of the school, village, and surrounding community.' The picture to the left has a few unidentified members of the Booster Club. Or, at least when I posted it on Facebook, no one wanted to claim that they were in the picture.

Lakeville Booster Club

Among the Booster Club projects were the school parking lot, playground equipment, lights for the ball diamond, drapes in the school gym, lockers, the ball diamond concession stand, and Booster Club Park. Their biggest project was aiding in the construction of the Lakeville Fire Department firehouse in 1952. They also purchased the fire siren. One of the activities I always enjoyed year after year was the ice cream festival. Still some of the best potato salad I have ever tasted. We have included the recipe.

FESTIVAL POTATO SALAD

Peel, boil, and cube 5 pounds of potatoes. Let cool.

Over the stove, cook the following together until thick: 3 beaten eggs, 2/3 cup sugar, 1 heaping T of flour, 1 t salt, 1 t dry mustard, ½ cup vinegar, and 1 cup water. Cook until it thickens, and then let cool. When cool, add ¾ cup Miracle Whip and enough evaporated milk to make one quart of sauce. Add to potatoes.

The Club also sponsored: Lakeville slow pitch softball, Lakeville Little League, and a Girls State participant. Sponsored events included: a meal for Teacher Appreciation Night, and the annual Halloween Party at the school. My sisters and I have many fond memories of parading around the gym in our costumes, hoping to be pulled into the middle to be presented a prize, and then heading down to the cafeteria for donuts and cider.

In 1976, the Booster Club built a float depicting George Washington crossing the Delaware. It was entered in several parades celebrating the US bicentennial. The float made its debut at the Nashville Memorial Day Parade on May 31, 1976. Among those pictured are Lester Welch, Dave Wigton, Howard Taylor, Dick Sprang, Jim Walters, and Deward Sprang.

In 1998, the club organized a celebration to commemorate Lakeville's 150th anniversary. Activities included a home-decorating contest, a parade, a chicken barbecue, a youth baseball tournament, a waterball competition, and a youth tractor pull. The chairman of the celebration was Howard Taylor, a lifelong resident. Over 40 entries

Souvenir medallion from Lakeville's Sesquicentennial in 1998

participated in the parade. The Grand Marshals of the parade, Velma Wigton, Paul and Vera Menchoffer, Lester Welch, Deward and Zola Spreng, Emerson and Vera Dilgard, and Bill Wagner rode on one of the floats. Handing out trophies to the winners were Doris Paullin, Lana Rush, and Pat Walters. After the parade, a ceremony was held at the school. Howard told about community achievements and Bill Wagner discussed the history of the community.

LAKEVIEW GARDEN CLUB

This club was organized on June 21, 1956. The group was a member of the Ohio Association of Garden Clubs since its beginning. The club's aim was to stimulate knowledge and love of gardening in the home and community. I remember the beautiful flower garden they planted and maintained at the intersection of Route 226 and 179, close to the Lakeville Booster Club Park. The garden club planned projects and programs for each month of the year. Some of their projects / programs over the years were therapy programs at Apple Creek Development Center, Christmas arrangements for the Millersburg Public Library, and programs / refreshments for the Holmes County Home residents. For one fund raiser, they sold flowering crabapple trees. Many blue ribbons were won over the years at the Holmes County Fair by both the club and by the individual members. Members pictured are: front – Mary Ann Sprang;

Lakeview Garden Club

middle row, left to right – Vera Menchhofer, Margaret Crawford, and Tina Mackey; kneeling behind Tina is Barb Long. Back row, left to right – Ceola Welch, Erma Gindlesberger, Judy Brooks, Mary Davenport, and Florence Maurer.

4-H

4-H has also been a popular club over the years. There were originally 2 clubs, the Lakeville Lassies for girls and the Lakeville Lakers for boys. The 2 clubs were combined in the late 1970s. The Lakeville Lakers was formed by Don and Barb Long and Dick and Mary Ann Sprang. Over the years, some of the advisors of the Lassies were Odessa Ferris, Bonnie Porter, Saundra Rhamey, and Doris Paullin. Many projects made it to the state level. And, to this day, every time I hear someone say "material", I remember Odessa telling us that it is fabric, not material. Many hours were spent at the Ferris home on cooking, sewing, and, occasionally, ripping out seams and sewing them again. Our end-of-the-season fashion show was always held at the Paullin home. In 1976 or 1977, the older girls of the Lassies club decided to take outdoor cookery as a group project. For the judging, we camped along the Mohican River and the judge came to us. Bonnie remembers one summer in the early 1980s when the Lakeville Lakers club was cruising around Lake O'Dell on the Walters' pontoon boat. Scott Rhamey and Bonnie's son, Scott Welch, had taken fishing as a project. The two boys decided to put a large sinker on the line and were attempting to cast it at a turtle. Today, the Lakeville Lakers represent the area with many varied projects. Another local group, formed in the early 2000s is the Lakeville Country Farmers. The group is led by Chris Gaines and the 45 members complete a full range of projects. They are active with community service projects, such as helping to clear tables at the annual Lakeville Fire Department chicken dinner.

21

Sports

Sports were a very popular part of Lakeville's history, baseball being one of the more popular. Lakeland Beach Park, on the east end of Lake O'Dell had a ball diamond. The Holmes County All Stars, a baseball team made up of men from all over the county, regularly played at the lake. In 1927, African American semi-pro, Satchel Paige, pitched at the diamond with the All Stars.

The Bloomer Girls from Chicago also frequented the lake to play baseball. Also challenging the local men, was a cultist team, the House of David from Benton Harbor, MI

Slow-pitch softball was very popular in the 1970s.

Lakeville Baseball team that George Denny played on. – *Submitted by his grandson, George Denny. He said picture is probably before 1920.*

Photo courtesy of Rex Parsons. Found in his grandfather's estate and was with family photos from his great-grandmother, Pearl Parsons.

Charley Collier – great-great uncle of Rex Parsons. – photo courtesy of Rex Parsons

Wayne County League Champs – September 1953. Front row – left to right – Dale Schmid, Walt Wachtel, John Anderson, Dave Wigton, Bob Shearer, Rex Dye. Back row – left to right – Curly Burgett, Howard Taylor, Jim Rhamey, Ted Acker, Don Gindlesberger, Mike Cramer. Not present – Harry McDaniel.

Lakeville's Robert "Curly" Burgett was one of the first inductees into the Holmes County Sports Hall of Fame on September 19, 1981. This is the bio from the program:

The late Robert "Curly" Burgett had the reputation as the best "long ball" hitter in local fast pitch softball circles. A 1940 graduate of Lakeville High School, he earned recognition as an outstanding basketball player, earning first team all-star recognition in his junior and senior years. Following high school, he entered the US Army and was seriously wounded during the Allied Invasion of Italy. Returning home after military service, Curly began playing with some of the stronger local teams and quickly developed into a tremendous hitter as well as a very fine third baseman. Later in his career, he began pitching and became one of the best in the entire area. Known as a fine competitor, he was always respected by his opponents as well as by his teammates. Curly was in the trucking business in Lakeville for many years until his appointment to the local post office where he continued to deliver mail until his recent death.

Curly was also one of the trustees who helped form the Holmes County Sports Hall of Fame on January 15, 1981. His help and guidance was greatly appreciated.

22

LAKEVILLE TIDBITS

Back in the 1830s Washington Township would not allow poor families to move to their community. They were told to "move on" out of the township. If you were a legal resident and became poor and unable to pay your bills, the Trustees sold all your belongings. They then paid the outstanding bills. If you still owed money you were sold to the highest bidder for 1 year to make up the debt. The trustee paid your temporary owner for your keep. The bidder (owner) would provide shelter, clothing and food. The indentured slave worked. Do you know that you were only worth $60.00-$80.00 a year back then? One poor lady was sold numerous years.

There have been reports of a spooky ghost train that rumbles down the tracks periodically. Questionably associated with the train wreck in 1890. If you lived close enough to the tracks every night you could see all the people sitting in the quite real passenger train that was heading east. I think it was between 9pm and 10pm.

It is reported that there is a sunken ferry at the bottom of Lake O'Dell. Although we asked John Rush and he stated that he had not heard of this rumor. So who knows?

There are old rumors that the pond located behind Lings/Lorentz home has no bottom. An owner once lost a piece of farm machinery or, as Lisa Ferris Miller stated, a wagon, in it that was never found. Also, was told that at one point they tried to measure the depth but were unable to find the bottom. I don't know if it is true but I have always wondered about it since my childhood.

A long time ago Hobos used to jump the train in Lakeville. One time when I was very small a Hobo came up the hill to me and Cindy while we were playing in her sandbox. I remember he asked for water so Cindy and I emptied our sand bucket and filled it with water. He drank it, grit and all, then went back down the hill.

Big Foot has been sighted recently west of Lakeville and was professionally investigated. This event was not disproven. But, that's another story.

It is reported by Bob Walters, Charles Lemon, and Rex Garnes that there was a tunnel that ran under the railroad tracks down where the old Depot used to be. Bob and Charles did not go in it but Charles's brother, Mike, did. Rex said that he hid a friend in it one time when he ran away from home. He also said that it was definitely manmade and carved out. He said that he always saw it when he went fishing with his dad as a child. My sisters and I decided this was road trip material. We set out on the hunt and parked at the bottom of Depot street. We crossed the track and searched. We actually did find a hole but it was grown over with weeds. Trusty Shelly went back to her car and got her pruning shears to cut away the briars. Frankly we didn't get far and it smelled of death. So, it might have been a ground hog hole. Here's a picture, you decide.

It was rumored that a famous mobster once stayed at the resort hotel. While there, he hid some money in a book. The money was never found.

John Rush said that back between 1915 and 1920 there was a train wreck in Lakeville that was transporting pigs. And, they were on the loose. His uncle, Ken Rush, who lived close to the tracks decided that since times were tough he would take a few hogs because he really wanted some bacon. He said there were many on the run. He captured 3 of them before the train detectives arrived but when his dad came home he had to return them to the site. No bacon for him.

Lisa Ferris Miller said that her dad Walt always told a story that back during Prohibition some booze was being smuggled on State Rt 3 and that they wrecked the vehicle down by Round Lake. Well, some nice men from town went to clean it up and the site was cleared. Lisa would ask her dad what ever became of the booze and all he would say is "We took care of it". End of story.

The low dipped section of road on state Route 3 between State Route 179 and before Round Lake was a corduroy road. Which means that logs were placed perpendicular to the direction of the road because the area was swampy.

Dick Porter said that his family found easels, pictures, and painting supplies above the corn crib. The Porter farm was previously owned by the O'Dell family and they rented out the space to a painter.

Norma (Miller) Threet remembers living on Horseshoe Alley from 1950 – 1957, except they called it Pigtail Alley at that time. They lived beside Cliff Horner. Cliff would catch turtles and make soup. Norma mowed his yard for 50 cents with a rotary mower.

The following articles were found in various newspapers. Sometimes they could be quite frank or graphic.

> For the Republican.
>
> Mr. Caskey—*Dear Sir*—False reports having been put in circulation against me in regard to the collection and payment of some Missionary Money in this place, permit me to give the public the facts in regard to it, so that they may judge as to the extent of my guilt as charged. Four persons including myself, subscribed $2.50 each to this fund, which money came into my hands. I handed the money over to the Rev. John Mitchell, with the names of the subscribers. He, by some means lost the list of names, and in reporting to Conference, did so from memory. He gave some credit for more than they subscribed, gave the given name of one wrong, and left one out entirely. He gave me the credit of subscribing more than I did. The amount of money was all accounted for, but the names of the subscribers, with the amount they subscribed, was not given correctly. As I have been very much abused and wronged in this matter, I have deemed it well enough to say thus publicly, that I am ready to prove all the facts above set forth, and hurl back the slanderous reports upon the heads of those who originated them. Yours &c., J. H. SNEDEKER.
> Lakeville, March 17, 1860.

Holmes County Republican – March 22, 1860

> **From Holmes County.**
>
> Akron, July 30.—Marriage is not quite a failure according to Grant Quick and Emma Evers, who were married by Justice Hoffman, yesterday. It was the third venture for each, Quick having lost one wife by death and one by divorce, while the Evers woman has been twice married and twice divorced.
>
> The Grant Quick above referred to is well known in the western part of this county, and formerly lived in the vicinity of Lakeville, says the Holmes County Farmer.

Akron Daily Democrat – August 9, 1901

Lakeville Damaged $15,000.

The village of Lakeville, near Wooster, suffered a $15,000 fire shortly before dinner Monday. An elevator owned by James Metcalf, the general store of Jacob Koppe and the residence of William Grow were destroyed. The postoffice, a store and the telephone exchange were badly damaged. Little insurance was carried.

Akron Daily Democrat – May 7, 1901

Three tramps broke into the dry goods store of J. L. Deyarman at Lakeville, about nine miles west of Wooster, on Saturday night. David Collier and a boy by the name of Butler were sleeping in the store, and the robbers seeing them began beating them over the face with clubs. They did not take any plunder and as yet have not been arrested, although the officers are on their track. Collier and Butler were pretty badly hurt.

The Democratic Press – January 22, 1880

NOTICE

IS hereby given that application will be made by the undersigned, who are the present proprietors and owners in fee simple, of the whole town of Lakeville, Holmes county, Ohio, to the Court of Common Pleas, of said Holmes county, at the next term thereof, for an order vacating said town; and that they claim title to a portion of said premises as the heirs of Isaac Bonnet, deceased, who was an assignee of the original proprietors, and the residue thereof as assignees of the assignees of said original proprietors, and that they are the present and only proprietors thereof.

Rebecca Bonnet, Mary Lovett, a married woman, by her next friend George Wolff, Isaac Bonnet, George Bonnet, and Henry Bonnet, minors, by their next friend George Wolff.

Dec. 16th, 1858—18w1.

Notice of vacancy of original site of Lakeville – Holmes County Republican – December 23, 1858

23

Lakeville Families

HARVEY BUTLER FAMILY

Troy Mae Lehr (1884-1972) was born in Clinton Township, Wayne County, on December 7, 1884, the daughter of Moses J. and Emily Walton Lehr. She was one of nine children. She married Harvey Jay Butler (1884-1948) and lived across from the Lakeville School for many years. Husband Harvey was a lifelong resident of Lakeville and spent 26 years as a teacher in the public schools. He was a carpenter by trade. Harvey died April 22, 1948. Harvey and Troy had two children, Vera (1907-1983) and George L (1911-1911).

Vera graduated from Lakeville School in 1926 and then from Ashland College in 1932 with a Bachelor's Degree in in Education. She retired in 1974 after spending 35 years in the Big Prairie and Nashville Schools. She lived in Lakeville for most of her life.

Troy Mae and Harvey Jay Butler – *from the collection of Deloris Horner*

DAVID COLLIER FAMILY

David Collier, ex-representative, was the son of Henry James Collier who emigrated from Adams County, Ohio, to Wayne County, in 1810. Henry was the first white settler in what is now Plain Township, and built a blockhouse on his farm at the foot of Old Fort Hill, about one mile east of Tylertown, called Lakefort.

David Collier was of Scotch-Welsh and German descent. He received his education in the common schools and at Vermillion Institute, Hayesville, Ohio.

David Collier and Granddaughters

He entered business at the age of eighteen as a grain, wool, and seed dealer at Lakeville. He had a farm near Lakeville and was interested in the Wooster & Mansfield Electric Railroad Company, of which he was Vice-President. He served six years as clerk and twelve years as Treasurer of Washington Township, and represented Ashland and Holmes Counties in the General Assembly as a Democrat from 1899 to 1901. He served in 17th Regiment, O.N.G., from 1884 to 1890, as Lieutenant of Company A, and for three years as Captain. He married Saphire Tope, May 3, 1874, had eight children, six boys and two girls, and was a member of the Methodist Church. – *Holmes County Ohio to 1985*

DAVID COLLIER AND FAMILY

CHARLES JR. AND BECKY DARR FAMILY

Charles was born February 18, 1943, in Stark Co. and attended Brewster School. In 1967 he joined the U S Army and was stationed in Germany. He married Becky Moyer on June 23, 1968. Charles enrolled at Waynedale High School in 1971 to finish his education, while Becky is an Ashland College graduate and is a licensed cosmetologist by trade. They lived in Lakeville in the house where her grandparents, John and Ruth Tope, raised their family around Horseshoe Alley.

Charles Darr Jr. Family

Charles and Becky have three daughters, Dawn (born July 5, 1971); Jennifer (born September 11, 1973); and Kerissa (born November 12, 1971). Charles and Becky currently live in Loudonville, Ohio.- *Becky Darr – early picture from Holmes County Ohio to 1985*

JOHN DOTY FAMILY

John H. Doty was born in 1875 in the neighborhood of Bloomfield, Holmes County, the son of Wilson and Jerusha Smith Doty. He was a school teacher, farmer, and one of the founders of the Washington Township Mutual Insurance Company. He became recognized as an authority on insurance matters, having served as secretary to that company for over thirty years.

John served as clerk of Washington Township from 1912 to 1927 and as a representative from Holmes County to the Ohio House of Representatives for two terms from 1928 to 1932. As a pastime, he raised dahlias and won many prizes for his efforts. John and his wife Osie Graven Doty, from Nashville, were the parents of two children, Frances and H. Eugene. John passed away in 1944 and Osie, in 1958. – *Holmes County Ohio to 1985*

FERRIS FAMILY

William Ferris was born on March 17, 1854, in Sheffield, England. In 1870, at age 16, he came to the USA with his parents and sister, Sarah, age 14. They arrived on a ship from Glasgow, Scotland, named Europa. Their ethnicity was listed as Scottish. His parents died from cholera in upstate New York. His sister went to live with relations in Massachusetts, while he came to Ohio to live with his relations, John Rainey. He married Mary Parcell on October 5, 1880. She was the daughter of James and Lydia Barnes Parcell. They had three children; Etta, who married Montford Eberhart; John; and Charles, who married Mary Wachtel. They moved from Lakeville to Dover in 1887, where Mary died from typhoid fever. William remarried, Catherine Wolf, and had the following children: Nina, Jennie, Amanda, Lydia and William. William died on January 15, 1904.

Charles and Mamie (Mary) Ferris – 1905

Etta Ferris married Montford Eberhart on June 3, 1902. Monty was a sawyer with his father. They had three children: Gilbert, who died young in a logging accident; Leora, who married Ralph McClure; and Arlene, who married Clarence Briggs. Etta was born March 16, 1881 and died March 7, 1945.

John Ferris was born May 4, 1883. He served in the end of the Spanish American War. He died November 24, 1902, in a railroad accident.

Floyd, Mamie, Boyd, and Walter Ferris

Kneeling, June, Standing – Odessa, Walter, Mamie holding BB Ferris, Viola, Charlie, and BB's mother, Mickey McCaskey. Missing is daughter Beatrice.

Odessa and Walter Ferris – 1944 Wedding picture

Charles Ferris was born January 26, 1887, and married Mary Wachtel on January 8, 1905. Charles was a custodian at the Lakeville School and was also a barber. His wife, Mary, ran the Star Telephone Office as a telephone operator. They had the following children: Beatrice, who married John Wagner; Viola, who did not marry; Geneva and Harry who both died young; Floyd, who married Clara Hiller; Boyd, who married Ruth McCaskey; Walter, who married Odessa Mellor; and June, who married William Kaylor.

Walter and Odessa Mellor were married on March 27, 1944. They had three daughters.

Peggy Gossman. Peggy has 2 children, Matthew and Jill. Matthew is married to Nikki. Jill and Ryan Duebber have 3 children – Josh, Sadie, and Eden.

Mary Odessa (Mimi), married Lou Loeber and they have two children, Melissa (Missy) and Grant. Missy and Matt Brewer have 3 children, Garrett, Cale, and Karly. Grant and Andriea Loeber also have 3 children, Ryleigh, Morgen, and Jaiden.

Lisa, and husband, Daryl Miller, have 2 children, Kristen and Lucas. Kristen and Joel Yoder have 2 children, Emelyn and Mila. Luke and his fiance, Sarah, have her son, Shawn. – *Submitted by Lisa Miller, B B Ferris, and William Wagner*

FAYE FRANKS

Faye Franks spent 50 years as a schoolteacher in the Holmes County area school rooms. She graduated from Killbuck High School in 1923 in a class of 10. At the end of a year of college and passing a teaching test, Franks taught at Butler School outside of Killbuck. She walked to and from school daily, often with wet and nearly frozen feet during the severe winter months. She received a salary of $100 a month, plus an additional $4 monthly for doing her own janitorial work.

Faye Franks

She often had a pot of soup brewing while she taught eight grades. Some of the students would bring cans of vegetables to add to the soup. Franks always brought the cocoa and some of the students brought the milk for the hot treat she served her students daily.

In 1939, Faye Jordan married Rod Franks, a teacher in the Lakeville school system. She left teaching for a year but at the outbreak of World War II resumed her teaching career because of the lack of available teachers.

The couple bought a home in Lakeville just on the east side of the school and remained there until 1964, moving back to Killbuck at that time. The home was then bought by Karl and Martha Schnittke. – *Holmes County Ohio to 1985*

GILLIAM FAMILY

Mary "Sellers" Gilliam was born October 1, 1919, in Loudonville (Ashland County) Ohio. Her parents were John and Cassie "Hannan" Sellers. The first time she was aware of Holmes County was when her mother told her about a farm in Glenmont that her grandmother "Sarah" Hannan owned and how once or twice each year grandmother Hannan walked to Glenmont to check on her farm and tenants there. Also, Mary remembers riding a train to O'Dells Lake amusement park for an exciting all day outing with her family. Mary graduated from Loudonville High School in 1937. In October 1939 she came to Lakeville to start her first job as a secretary to John Doty at Washington Mutual Insurance Company. She lived in a tourist home in Lakeville owned by the Sharr sisters "Mary and Lizzie". In December 1941(shortly after the bombing at Pearl Harbor) she met Henry C. "Dick" Gilliam who at that time was living at Long Lake in Holmes County. He was employed at Mansfield Tire & Rubber Company and during the war worked seven days a week building tires for defense, much of the work devoted to experimental tires. On May 3, 1943, they were married and shortly thereafter bought a home at O'Dells Lake and took up residence there. On February 16, 1945, they became parents of a son, Richard, and on September 14, 1947, became parents of a daughter, Jacquelyn. Henry Gilliam died on September 25, 1958. The family continued to live at O'Dells Lake. Dick and Jacquie attended school in Lakeville and Big Prairie, Dick graduating from Big Prairie High School and Jacquie with the first graduating class at West Holmes High School in 1965. Mary retired in 1982 from Crown Divisions of The Allen Group, Inc. in Wooster where she was employed as a secretary. She has lived in Wooster since August 1969 when she sold their home at O'Dells Lake in Lakeville. *Submitted by Mary Gilliam – 1985 to Holmes County Ohio to 1985*

Henry C. and Mary Gilliam

. Update – Mary Gilliam died on January 22, 2000 at the age of 80 and is buried in Sandridge Cemetery in Loudonville, Ohio.

ERMA GINDLESBERGER

Erma was born in 1901, the daughter of Albert and Mary (Findlay) Logsdon. She was a 1919 graduate of Millersburg High School and a 1926 graduate of Oberlin College. In 1965, she received her librarian degree from Kent State University.

She had taught school for 37 years in Ohio, with all but two years in Holmes County. She had taught English and Latin at Lakeville and Big Prairie high schools and was a librarian for eight years at West Holmes High School.

She married Waldo Gindlesberger. He died in January 1942. They had three sons, Richard, Donald, and Albert Wade.

Erma made her home in Lakeville, across from the school house, for 52 years. She was well known for her beautiful gardens, especially her roses. She passed away in Loudonville in 1995 at the age of 93.

HALL FAMILY

Adolphus Hall (1856-1922) was married to Carrie Elder Hall (1854-1944). He was a hard-working man; and it is told that a hired hand of his would turn the clock forward at noon so that he would be ensured of being released from work that day at a decent hour. Thusly, Carrie could not understand why her afternoon went so fast! She was such an over-modest woman that, when about to give birth to son Floyd, she locked herself in the bedroom so that no one might witness the birth; but the door had to be broken down so that Floyd, at twelve pounds, might be born with the doctor's help. Floyd, and his wife, Martha Mae Spreng Hall, both attended Fairview School and married in 1911. They lived on the Hall home place and one other farm in Holmes County, then settled across the road from Floyd's birthplace, Fairview Farm. It was here in 1941 that Martha lost her right hand in a corn husking machine. Husband Floyd was so upset over her hand loss that he quickly disposed of her pedal organ thinking she could no longer play it. Martha learned to use her left hand to keep house and was very careful to never let anyone notice her missing hand. Their second born, Vera Spreng Hall, later married Paul Menchhofer. – *Holmes County Ohio to 1985*

KENNETH R. HEIMBERGER FAMILY

Kenneth R. Heimberger built his residence on the Calico Road in Washington Township just across the road from where his great grandfather, Jacob Heimberger's, log home was located.

Jacob Heimberger came to Washington Township from Alsace. Kenneth married Bessie M Strang, from Danville, in 1942. Soon Kenneth was serving Uncle Sam as a United States Navy radioman aboard a destroyer in the Atlantic and later in the Pacific. Kenneth and Bessie had four children.

Kenneth worked in the construction business as a carpenter for about 30 years. He retired from this to help Bessie operate Calico Greenhouse at their home on Calico Road.

Kenneth R. Heimberger Family

After several years in the greenhouse business, they branched out into the floral shop business with his shop in Loudonville and her shop, Calico Florist, in Millersburg.

In August of 1983, they sold both shops and moved to Florida. – *Holmes County Ohio to 1985*

JOHN W. HORN

John W. Horn, a native of Reedsburg, Wayne Co., Ohio, where he was born January 31, 1856. He is the son of George W. and Susan Sellinger Horn. His father was a native of Adams Co. PA., and his mother of Switzerland.

Mr. Horn was educated in Reedsburg and Blachleyville district schools in Wayne County. He began farming at an early age which he followed with stock raising and later conducted a machinery business and a grain elevator. The grain elevator was located in Lakeville

Mr. Horn was a Democrat and a member of the school board for five years. He was a member of the Maccabees Lodge located at Plimpton, (Lakeville) Ohio.

On March 1887, he married Miss Mary Jan Griffeth, daughter of Alexander and Elizabeth Buffenmeier Griffeth. The following children were born. Wayne G. born July 26, 1888, Harvey Kay born December 27, 1890, Vere born November 26, 1893, John Lloyd born July 30, 1896, Glen A. born June 30, 1900, and Helen M. born January 22, 1904.

He was a member of English Lutheran Church and resided in Lakeville, his post office Plimpton, Ohio. – *Holmes County Ohio to 1985*

HARVEY K. HORN

Harvey K. Horn son of John and Mary Horn born at Horns Corners December 27, 1890. He was second oldest of six children. The family moved to Plimpton, Ohio, now known as Lakeville in 1894. Father Horn and Ervin Smyser opened a hardware store and grain elevator. Harvey joined his father in the business at a very young age after the dissolution of the Horn-Smyser partnership. He fell in love with a young lady, Nellie Ellis, who was working in a millinery store. Many trips were made to Craigton by Harvey during their courtship. They were married in 1915 and set up housekeeping in Lakeville. Three children were born to this union.

Wayne Gray in 1915, Walter Eugene in 1918, and Mary Louise in 1920. Harvey died in May of 1981 and is buried in Ormond Beach, Florida. – *Holmes County Ohio to 1985*

WALTER EUGENE HORN

Walter Eugene Horn was the second of three children born to Nellie and Harvey Horn. He graduated from Lakeville High School in 1936. Walter attended Wooster College majoring in pre-med courses. To help defray the cost of his expenses, he stayed with an aunt who operated a rest room on Market Street. He took his medical training at Ohio State, graduating Cum Laude. Walter joined the U.S. Army. His internship was spent in Guatemala, sent to Germany where he served in the Medical Corps until 1946. His German wife, Gertrude, accompanied him back to the U.S. Walter took further training, specializing in dermatology. A practice was set up in Portsmouth, Ohio, where he continued to practice until his death of questionable circumstances in December 1954. He is buried in Fairview Cemetery. – *Holmes County Ohio to 1985*

WAYNE GRAY HORN

Wayne Gray Horn born in Lakeville, April 3, 1915, was the eldest of three children. His childhood was spent in Lakeville, surrounded by loving parents, visiting grandmother Gray at Craigton. Sports occupied most of his time through his school years playing as catcher on the Lakeville baseball team, and basketball team. He graduated from Lakeville High School in 1933 and joined his father in the hardware and grain elevator. In 1941, he married Alice Swanson, a nurse who worked at the City Hospital in Wooster. They lived in Lakeville until 1942 when Wayne enlisted in the Army as the United States was at war with Germany and Japan. He took basic training in Fort Bragg, NC, then was sent to Oklahoma where Lois was born June 26, 1942. In 1943 the

Wayne Horn Family

Wisconsin National Guard sent Wayne to Africa and on to Italy. He served as forward observer for the heavy artillery where he had emergency surgery, bringing an end to his Army duty. He was sent back to Cleveland Veterans Hospital and discharged in 1945. He then came back to Lakeville where he rejoined the hardware and elevator.

Two more children were born to Wayne and Alice. James M. December 25, 1945 and Dennis December 10, 1951. Wayne took over as sole owner of Horn Hardware and Elevator and a tavern was added in 1946 known as "Horns Bomb Shelter." The business was sold in 1949 and Wayne became a rural carrier and raised beef cattle and hogs. He resigned as mail carrier. Wife Alice became a partner in Horn Nursing Home in Wooster with mother Nellie Horn. In 1960, Wayne sold the farm. They purchased the Beeson Clinic, converting it into a nursing home. A few years later, the Hatfield property was purchased, an addition added, bring the location to 78 beds combined with a small home of 20 beds on Market Street, and a 44 bed home on Bever Street. Wayne was a warm individual who loved life and people and continued as owner-administrator of Horn Nursing Homes until his death in January of 1968. He is buried in Fairview Cemetery. – *Holmes County Ohio to 1985*

HELEN KNOX

Helen Knox was a quick-to-smile-and-laugh woman who loved kids. She lived in the last house on 3rd Street off of County Road 100. She would take us kids in her boat over to the island in the middle of Lake O'Dell to play.

She worked at Diamonite and hung wallpaper. She was married to "Mouse" Mosher, then Earl, with whom she had a son. She loved her grandchildren. Her last husband was Eddie who took her to Florida to live for the rest of her life. – *Submitted by Becky Moyer Darr*

GEORGE KOPP, SR

George Kopp, Sr., (1830-1906) was a native of Buchenburg, Baden, Germany, emigrating to America in 1851, resided in Ashland County several years, and moved to Holmes County in 1875. George had four sons, George Martin, John Franklin, Jacob Benjamin, and Simon Peter. He had one daughter, Sarah Caroline. John Franklin (1860-1950) was father to Ralph Hugo (1888-1968) Ralph was the father of Paul Kopp. (1913-1984). Ralph ran a general store in Lakeville in the early 1900s.

SIMON P. COPP AND FAMILY

Simon Peter owned a home on Depot Street, which was later sold to Kenneth and Florence Rush.

George Sr., who was deaf, died in 1906. He was struck and instantly killed by a Pennsylvania train while crossing the tracks to go to the saloon. - *Information provided by Rita Kopp*

JACOB BENJAMIN KOPP

Jacob Benjamin Kopp, born July 1, 1868, near Loudonville, Ashland County, Ohio, son of George Kopp, Sr., native of Baden, Germany, and his mother was a native of Alsace, Germany. George emigrated to America in 1851, resided in Ashland County several years, moving to Holmes County in 1875. Jacob Kopp was educated in the Lakeville Schools. He was a farmer and a dealer in stock, after conducting a general store. On March 27, 1895, he married Minnie Irene Kantzer. He was a Democrat in politics, and belonged to the German Lutheran Church. He resided in Lakeville, Ohio. – *Holmes County Ohio to 1985*

Jacob and Minnie Kopp

JOHN KRIEGER FAMILY

John Krieger, blacksmith and wagon-maker, was born in Bueswiler, Elsass, France, on June 24, 1855. His father was George Krieger, and his mother, Margaret Pfister, both natives of Elsass, both of whom died there.

Mr. Krieger was educated in Elsass, France, and started to work in a paint shop at twelve years of age. He afterwards learned the blacksmith trade and set up shop in Lakeville.

JOHN KRIEGER AND FAMILY

On November 12, 1874, he married Miss Sarah Derrenberger, daughter of Michael and Catherine Richert Derrenberger. Of the marriage, four children were born as follows: Josephine L., born September 9, 1875; Frank E., born

January 16, 1877 (died January 5, 1879); Theresa M., born September 11, 1883; and Dudley B., born October 10, 1898.

LEMON FAMILY

Charles "Bud" Lemon, wife Mary, and family lived first on Horseshoe Alley. In the 1970s, they moved to the next to last house on Depot Street.

Charles "Bud" Lemon, wife Mary, sons Mike and Charles

Daughter – Kathy Lemon

LONG FAMILY

Left to Right: John Andrew Long, Donald Long, Barbara Long, and Amy Long

Donald and Barbara Long called Lakeville home for twenty-five years. They moved to Lakeville in 1973 after Don became secretary-treasurer to Washington Mutual Insurance Company. Barbara had Lakeville connections because her mother was Farrell Wigton Brown and her grandparents were Zane and Golda Wigton. Don and Barbara had two children, Amy and John Andrew. They resided in the two-story farm house (beside the once Washington Mutual Insurance company building) across the road from the home that Barbara's grandparents had built. Don worked at Washington Mutual for fourteen years before leaving to become self-employed. Barbara worked at Lakeville School for nine years after completing her degree in education. They were active in the Lakeville Booster Club and started the

Lakeville Lakers 4-H Club with Dick and Mary Ann Sprang. Don helped coach the BP-L Little League for several years. Barb was a member of the Lakeville Garden Club. Amy and Andy were active in school and 4-H. At the end of twenty-five years, they moved to Nashville to a home they built on land from her parents' farm. *Submitted by Barbara Long*

ALBERT LOZIER

Lozier Family

Albert Scott Lozier, eldest son of Esli J. and Ellen (Wiggins) Lozier, was born November 9, 1869, in the log house on Township Rd 273, also known as the Calico Road, in Washington Township near Lakeville, Ohio.

He went to Akron, Ohio, in early 1892 to work. On June 12, 1892, he married Daisey M. Kelser of Washington Township in Akron, where they lived until returning to live on the township road near Lakeville. Shortly afterward, they purchased a nearby farm from Aunt Lib Lozier. Their two sons were born in the small house on this farm and raised there. In 1919, they built a new home on the farm, where they lived until retiring from farming in 1931. They moved to Wooster Road, Loudonville, Ohio. Scott Lozier died in 1949 and his wife, Daisy, died in 1952.

Their three children were: **Ruby Ellen** 1894 – 1983; **Rodger Hugo** 1895-1982; and **Reno Eugene** 1896 – 1988. – *Submitted by Mrs. Richard W. Lozier to Holmes County Ohio to 1985*

ESLI J. LOZIER

"Let me live in my house by the side of the road and be a friend of man."

The above verse is from the poem "The House By the Side of the Road" by Sam Walter Foss and was a favorite of Esli J. Lozier and was a part of his funeral service.

In Washington Township near Lakeville, Ohio, is Township Road 273, also known as the Calico Road and about halfway between Route 39 to the west and the Lakeville / Nashville Road. There, a three-level log house built against the hillside alongside the township road, is where Esli J. Lozier was born November 19, 1842. He lived there his entire life, except for the period he served in Lincoln's Army in Company K, O.V.I., 166th Regiment.

It was said the house was built in 1815 near the spring, where there would be plenty of water, and with the help of friendly Indians in the area, who also had free use of the water. Esli would sit on a bench under a huge shade tree in front of the house and visit with folks stopping to let their horses drink from the watering trough at the spring. The house was still standing in 1984, but badly damaged by vandals.

September 17, 1868, Esli married Ellen W. Wiggins, who was born about a mile from the Lozier home, April 20, 1846. She lived in the log house until she died in 1929. Esli died in 1924. They are buried in the Loudonville, Ohio, cemetery. The couple had four children: Leo L., Martha Lenora (Nora), Medora (Dora), and Albert Scott. – *Submitted by Mrs. Reno E. (Ferne) Lozier, Sr to Holmes County Ohio to 1985*

Esli Lozier Homes

DON MACKEY FAMILY

Don Mackey

The Mackey family has deep roots in Holmes County. Don's ancestors originally moved here from Pennsylvania in 1809. They returned to Pennsylvania during the War of 1812 and returned to Holmes County in 1814. Don's parents were Glen and Mildred who farmed and lived near Big Prairie all their lives. Don was one of seven children.

Don married Kathryn Miller on September 11, 1960. They added four children to the family: Belinda, Donna, Gail, and David, all in the 1960s thru 1970. They have called Lakeville home for many years, having lived in the former school house building outside of Lakeville and later moving next door to the former home of Kathryn's parents, Mark and Olive Miller. *Holmes County Ohio to 1985*

THE CECIL MARMET FAMILY

Cecil came to Lakeville in 1916 to work at the Lakeville Hotel. There he met and married Mae Regne. They raised three children at the hotel, Paul, Eleanor and Marjie.

Paul married Ruby Knox in 1940. During this union he served as a Corporal medic with the 83 infantry (Thunderbolt) Division in Normandy during WWII. When he returned from the war, he and Ruby moved into a home in Lakeville located in the Horseshoe Alley. They had three children Dwaine, Linda Sue Ellen and Rosa Lee. Before the birth of their youngest daughter they moved to a home on State Route 179 across from the tracks. (Current home of Dick and Bonnie Porter) Paul worked at Diamonite and was a hunter, trapper and fisherman. Ruby died in 1963 of a brain aneurysm. Paul later remarried and moved near Glenmont.

Linda Marmet married Lloyd Young and they lived in the home on State Route 179. They had one son Michael. They eventually moved closer to his place of employment Rubbermaid. Dwaine married Darlene Parker and they purchased the home on State Route 179 where they raised two sons' Randy and Rick. Rosa Lee became a nurse and married Dan Leonard and had two daughters Sara and Hanna- *Submitted by Becky Moyer Darr*

PAUL EDGAR MENCHHOFER FAMILY

Paul Edgar Menchhofer was born February 24, 1908, the second child of George and Gertrude Menchhofer above the grocery store they owned in Loudonville. Paul was a farmer with his father in Ashland County and then farmed in Holmes County from 1938 forward. Because he farmed with horses at first, twice they "got away" from him and came charging home by themselves, jumping over barnyard gates and smashing them! Since the horse collars were still hanging in his barn when grandson Michael was young, he commented that "Grandpa used that stuff when he used to be Amish!"

Paul's wife, Vera Spreng Hall Menchhofer, was born the second child of Robert Floyd Hall and Martha Mae Spreng Hall on April 10, 1916, in the farm house standing at the corner of State Route 3 and State Route 179 in Holmes County. She graduated from Lakeville School in 1934, where she was a member of the girls' basketball team. Her paternal grandparents were Adolphus Hall and Carrie Elder Hall. (See Hall Family History). Vera's maternal grandparents were C. John Spreng and Josephine Kick Spreng. (See Spreng Family History).

Paul and Vera Menchhofer

Children born to Paul and Vera are Raymond Edgar Menchhofer (July 1, 1941) and Mary Ann Menchhofer Sprang (August 2, 1945), who resided with her husband, Richard, within walking distance of her parents.- *Submitted by Richard Sprang to Holmes County Ohio to 1985*

ROBERT J. AND MARY A. MOYER FAMILY

Mary Alice Tope, daughter of John and Ruth Raby Tope, was born in Lakeville on October 15, 1927, and was married to Robert J. "Pete" Moyer, born November 5, 1927, in Bertrand, Michigan. They were married at Sheppard Field, Texas, on March 23, 1946.

Pete served in the U.S. Air Force and they lived in Texas until he was shipped to the Philippines and Mary returned to Lakeville to live. Pete joined her in Lakeville after his discharge in 1947.

Robert and Mary Moyer

Pete worked at the Loudonville Flexible Co., while Mary worked at Diamonite in Shreve and then later at the Flexible Co.

Both Pete and Mary were active in the community, both contributing to the many organizations in Lakeville. Pete served as Captain and later Chief of the Lakeville Fire Department. He was a Special Deputy Officer during the "Bomb Shelter" days. Mary was an early member of the Lakeville Fire Department Auxiliary and the Lakeville Garden Club. Also, she served as a Red Cross Instructor for many years. Pete's hobbies were small engine repair and wood working. Mary's hobbies were flower gardening and also wood working.

They welcomed their only child, Becky on April 1, 1947. She married Charles Edward Darr Jr. on June 23, 1968. *Holmes County Ohio to 1985*

JOHN PAULLIN FAMILY

John and Doris (Wachtel) Paullin moved to Lakeville in 1952 with their three young children, Penny, Chuck and Jane. Jane's twin sister Janice died at birth.

They went on to have three more daughters, Deb, Dianne and Nancy.

They lived in Lakeville until their passing, John in 2009 and Doris in 2014.

John was a self-employed milk hauler with Paullin Milk Cartage where he retired in 1995 after hauling milk for over 50 years. He was an active member of the Lakeville Volunteer Fire Department, The Lakeville Booster Club and played on the Lakeville Men's slow pitch softball team for many years. He was a member of the Lakeville United Methodist Church.

Doris was a homemaker famous for her pies and home-made cinnamon rolls. She later worked for Haudenschild Insurance for several years before moving to Washington Mutual Insurance in Lakeville from which she retired after several years.

She was a 4-H leader for several years for the Lakeville Lassies 4-H Club.

Doris was a very active member of the Lakeville United Methodist Church. She was choir director, Sunday school teacher, Bible school teacher and was a member and officer of the Ladies Aid.

Doris was also founder and director of JAM (Jesus And Me). This was an after-school program for area kids led by Doris and Ruth Miller.

John and Doris would host Friendly Town Kids for several years, and at one time Doris was the recruiter for Holmes County. This was a program where Cleveland inner city children would come and stay with a host family for a week during the summer. For many kids, this was their first time out of the city. One summer they hosted 5 children in their home. They knew the need and didn't want any kids left behind that wanted to spend a week out of the city. Several children that they hosted would return for visits, even after they were too old for the program. That's how much they loved coming to spend time with John and Doris.

John and Doris lived in the same house in Lakeville and were married for over 60 years before John passed away. Their son, Chuck, still resides in Lakeville with his wife in the house right next door to where he grew up with "Mom and Dad" and his 5 sisters. Chuck was also a Milk Hauler for Paullin Milk Cartage for several years before retiring. Penny lives in Danville and is retired from Danville School Systems after more than 30 years. Jane lives in Loudonville with her husband Mike, who retired from Mansfield Sanitary after over 30 years. Deb is in Las Cruzes NM with her husband John, and has been employed by the Las Cruzes School System for over 30 years. Dianne has worked for Rubbermaid for over 30 years and lives in Wooster. And Nancy resides in Killbuck with husband Ed and is a Speech Pathologist for Newcomerstown School System. *Submitted by Dianne Paullin Bell*

CHARLES AND BETTY PORTER

Charles and Betty Porter Family

Charles and Betty lived on the east end of Lakeville on the old O'Dell farm. The house was well over a hundred years old, making it one of the older homes in the community.

Chuck was the younger son of John and Marie Smetzer Porter of Shreve. When their parents passed away, Chuck and his brother and sister made their home with their mother's sister, Laura Smetzer Richey. Mom and Dad (Roy) Richey had five children: Mel, Cotta, Roy Jr., Jean, and Rita.

They were married in 1952 in Big Prairie and then bought the O'Dell farm in February 1960, and moved to Lakeville. Chuck graduated from Big Prairie in 1951. Chuck and Betty met while both were working on the Paul Richey farm. They had to crawl on their knees to weed the onions, and in the fall they harvested potatoes the same way. Betty and her sister,

Freda, later detassled corn on Jim Shane's hybrid seed corn farm. Betty came with her family to Ohio from Kentucky in 1942. Her father bought their family home from the Charles Bauer family at Lakeville. Betty also worked in the cafeteria at Lakeville School.

The Porters had three children, Richard, Rhonda, and Charles, Jr. Dick is married to Bonnie Rice Welch and they have 4 children: Scott, Laura, John, and Robbie. Rhonda married Ted Morris and they have 3 children: Micheal, Broc, and Amanda. Charlie lives in the family home in Lakeville. – *Holmes County Ohio to 1985*

Front – Bonnie and Richard (Dick) Porter. Back row – their children, John Porter, Scott Welch, Laurie Porter Vales, and Robert Rice.

JULIUS LOUIS REGNE FAMILY

Julius Louis Regne was born April 7, 1868, in Bern, Switzerland, the son of Joseph Regne and Philomene Carty Regne.

Julius married Adaline "Addy" Schafer on December 26 1892.

Without formal education, Julius was an excellent businessman. He was in the farming and mining business and for a time was engaged in the drilling of oil wells. Julius was well known for his favorite expression, "I may be wrong, but that's the way I see it." Julius purchased the Lakeview Hotel on O'Dell's Lake in Lakeville, Ohio (formerly Plimpton) from John Rush in 1909, which he also ran. The hotel was sold in 1929; however, he maintained possession until 1934 He later moved to Loudonville, Ohio, and opened a café.

Julius L. Regne Family

Julius and Adaline had six children; (1) Unnamed male, died two days after birth; (2) Mae Beatrice, married Cecil Marmet; (3) Walter Edward, died shortly before his fifth birthday; (4) Cecilia "Celie" Agnes, married Jack Kloverdale and later Cyrus Wheeler; (5) Edna Alice, died at age one; and (6) Alvin Titus, married Gladys Held. *Holmes County Ohio to 1985*

THE RUSH FAMILY

One of the most influential families in the history of Lakeville would have to be the Rush family. They were essentially the builders of Lakeville, having built homes, three hotels, boats, furniture, the ice house, and train depot. They also built the grandstand at the Wayne County Fairground in Wooster, Ohio. The Rush family also had a knack for moving buildings when needed.

John Rush Sr. was the son of Jacob and Margaret Huffman-Rush who came to America around 1830, settling first in Wooster, Ohio and then moving to the north side of Lake O'Dell close to where eventually Lakeville (or at that time known as Plimpton) would become a town.

Rush Family

It is assumed that Jacob built the home they lived in which also served as a hotel with a bar in the basement. In 1870, Jacob built the fifty-room hotel and amusement park, turning the west end of Lake O'Dell into the Recreational Area of the Midwest with thousands of people coming to enjoy the lake and its amenities. This hotel was known as Lakeview Hotel and later another Rush hotel was built on a hill with a partial road in front of it (later becoming County Road 100) with Lloyd Horn operating the Castle Inn Hotel. The Rush family built all the boats at the hotel, each of them named after one of his children. Boats could be rented out and a swimming area was provided for hotel guests and visitors. The park also had a steamboat and a boat for the band from Nashville, Ohio, who would play music on the boat that would drift across the lake. Around 1915, Oak Park was built for families to enjoy the concession stand, pavilion with picnic tables, benches and the swimming area.

John Rush Sr. married Mary Crumlick and had six children, one being John Rush Jr. After the death of Mary, John Rush married Margaret Dewitt.

John Rush Jr. married Ellen Kirkendall and had ten children; Verd, Clovis, Clarence, Kenneth, Bessie, Warren, Elza, Dallas, Grover, and Aeolus. Around the time of Kenneth's birth, John Jr. became the manager of The Consolidated Ice Company. Many of the Rush children worked at the Ice Company, Kenneth was only a teenager when he was promoted to foreman and maintenance man of the company.

On June 12, 1920, Kenneth Rush married Mary Florence Glasgo from Millersburg, Ohio. Kenneth continued to work at the ice house until 1924 when the ice house was closed down due to the spreading use of electricity, putting over one hundred men out of work. After the demise of the ice business, Kenneth and his siblings started their own contracting business, successfully building many commercial and residential buildings. Kenneth and Florence lived in Lakeville on Depot Street in the former Simon Peter Kopp home, where he pursued his knowledge of woodworking as a hobby, even building a small water wheel designed after the large wheel at the Grist Mill in Millbrook.

CHRISTIAN SPRENG, SR. FAMILY

Christian Spreng, Sr., was born January 1, 1777 in Germany and served with the French Army under Napoleon, suffering much hardship as a soldier

He survived the Russian Campaign and also a wound made by a musket ball passing through his lungs. Finally, he ended a 21-year military career, on the battlefield of Waterloo, in June 1815 when Napoleon surrendered.

He then married Magdelana Nuesp and, in 1828, brought her and their 5 children to

Christian Sprang Family

America. They settled in Washington Township, Holmes County.

For some unknown reason, Christian Spreng, Jr., changed his last name to SPRANG. Perhaps it was to distinguish himself from his father since they farmed in the same community.

Another son, Jacob Sr., married Catherine Yunt and reared 8 children in Holmes County. Jacob's trade was sawing and threshing.

One of Jacob's sons, Christian John, (C. John), wed Josephine Kick. To this union was born Ada, Harry, Ellen, Carl, Martha, Ethel, and Carrie.

John was a prominent farmer staying close to his church and community. He invested in the Calico Railroad which was to run from Lakeville southwest through the valley near Bill Stitzlein's farm on toward State Route 39. This, however, never came to pass. He and Carl worked winters at the ice house at O'Dells Lake cutting high blocks of ice for sale to homes in the area.

The children attended Fairview School. Carl often told stories of how "the roads were so muddy that it took 2 teams of horses to pull the school wagon."

The school was located near Boyland Hill and was closed during their learning years so they were to go into Plimpton (Lakeville) to complete their education. However, John would not permit it. His reason being that it was unsafe to send children to a wild and worldly place like Lakeville. They might "learn things."

Harry and Carl Spreng

Dark days fell upon the family when brother Harry died of pneumonia in March of 1907 at the age of 19. Then, on December 26, 1914, John was killed while crossing the tracks at Lakeville after unloading a wagon of stock, leaving his widow and 6 children to carry on the farming. The girls worked along with their one brother, Carl, to keep the family together

Daughter Martha married Robert Floyd Hall. Their daughter, Vera Spreng Hall, went on to marry Paul Menchhofer.- *Submitted to Holmes County Ohio to 1985 by Paul & Marilyn Spreng*

THE HOWARD TAYLOR FAMILY

Howard (Mac) Taylor was born July 13th, 1927 near Big Prairie, Ohio. He was the son of Harold and Helen Taylor. He married Helen Graham on December 25th, 1948. He served in the U.S Army in World War II. He was part of MacArthur's Color Guard and he was involved in guarding Hirohito's Empire. Back in his homeland he was busy as an active member of the Lakeville United Methodist Church. He was a Sunday School teacher for many years. Mac was always able to keep young teenagers interested in the word of God with just a few fishing stories thrown in. He was an active member of the Lakeville Booster Club and organized the historic 150th Anniversary Lakeville parade.

Mac was an avid fisherman and he would often share his bounty of perch from Lake Erie with folks in Lakeville. Many fish fries were held at the Lakeville Fire Department thanks to him. Mac and Helen had four children: Bob, Don, Jim and Susie. Howard tragically died on February 6th 2001 while ice fishing on Lake Erie. This was a tragic time for all the people in Lakeville as he was truly loved by all who knew him.

THE JAMES EDWIN THOMPSON FAMILY

James Edwin Thompson was born March 10th, 1868 in Washington Township, Holmes county. His parents were John Elder Thompson and Elizabeth Ann Rainey. He grew up in Washington Township and attended the public schools there. At the age of 28 he opened a mercantile business in Plimpton (Lakeville). He sold groceries, tobacco, cigars and notions. In 1897 he was appointed Postmaster under President McKinley. James married Coral Francis Nouse. They had one daughter. James was a member of the Methodist Episcopal Church, Knights of Pythias and Modern Woodmen of America.

THE CORWIN TOPE FAMILY

Corwin Tope was born on 5/19/1876. He married Lucy Donley on 10/28/1896. They lived on an 80-acre farm on township road 466 just outside of Lakeville. They raised three children: John, Ocy and Floyd.

It is written that Corwin was an ill-tempered man who believed in hard work even if you were only a child of 6 years old. His philosophy was "if you don't work, you don't eat". Even his grandchildren were not spared of work as they were required to kill bumble bees in the fields with special paddles.

It is said that his wife Lucy was his opposite. She was quiet and would sing hymns while she worked. She was an excellent cook and enjoyed quilting. All luxury items in the home were for guests only and the children slept on straw mattresses.

John was born 11/24/1897. In 1918 he married Ruth Raby. They had eight children: William, Carrie, John Jr. Paul, Calvin, Lucille, Mary, Don and Clara Rose. John was employed by the PA Railroad as a repairman. He worked there for 43 years till he retired. John and Ruth eventually divorced and he married Elsie Hollett. The two youngest children from the prior marriage were taken by their mother and eventually adopted by other families. The oldest child (William) lived and worked on his grandfather (Corwin's) farm. John Jr lived with his Uncle Floyd and farmed. Elsie raised 4 of the children as her own. John and Elsie lived on Horse Shoe Alley in Lakeville. After John retired, he kept busy sharpening mower blades, fixing mowers and other assorted repairs in his shop close to his home.

John and Ruth Tope

Ruth and all eight children

Back – Ocy Tope Beck, Grandma Livingston, Ruth Raby Tope. Front – Bill Tope, Carrie Tope, and John (Steve) Tope

Frank and Ocy Tope Beck holding granddaughter Barbara – January 1958

John and Elsie

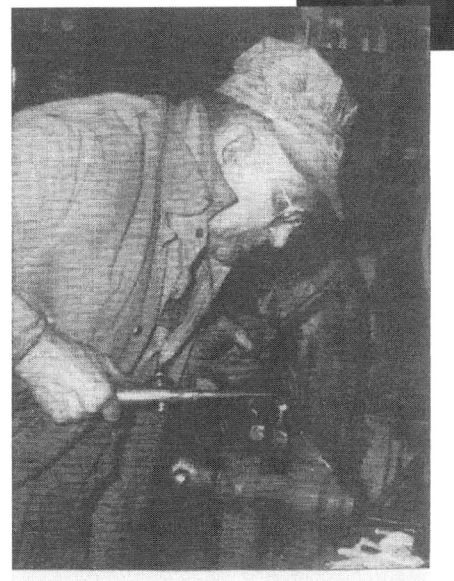

"Old John"

LLOYD WILLIAM TOPE FAMILY

Lloyd William Tope was born in 1909. He graduated from Lakeville high school. and married Faye Harris in 1932. Lloyd was a farmer and also worked for a gas company running casing pipe. He was a Washington Township trustee for 18 years. He was the president of Lakeville Booster Club. He and Faye had two sons, Leo Wayne and Carl Wilbur. Leo married Janice McQuire in 1958. They have three children, Mary Lou, Carol, and Wayne. Carl (Dud) Tope was born in 1937. He married Norma Jean Miller and they have 2 children, Carl Wesley and Cynthia.

Cindy, Wesley, Wayne, Janice, Carol, Leo, Mary Lou, Faye

Faye, Lloyd

Leo and Janice

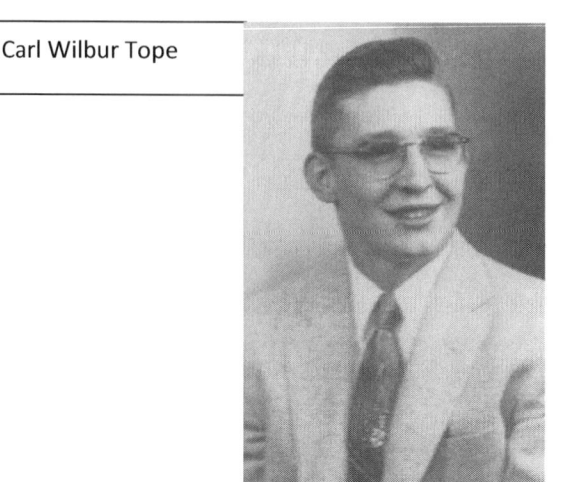

Carl Wilbur Tope

CHARLES WACHTEL FAMILY.

Charles Wachtel was born August 28, 1861, and died October 14, 1933. Charles first married Katherine Emmons, daughter of Peter and Susan Force Emmons, on December 21, 1882. They had the following children: Ernest, who married Iva Carpenter; Mary, who married Charles Ferris; John, who married Grace Appleman; Lula, who died young; and Fern, who married Roy Powell. Katherine died May 16, 1893, from child birth problems.

Charles married a second time to Ellen Boley, daughter of Jacob and Sarah Lehr Boley, on March 1, 1898. They had the following children: Harriet, who married Charles Shearer; Lillie, who died young; Dorothy, who married Howard Rhamey; Donald, who married Bertha Fouch; and Olive, who married Mark Miller. Charles was a farmer in the Big Prairie and Lakeville area. Ellen was born in June 1869, and died February 18, 1952.- *Holmes County Ohio to 1985*

JAMES WALTERS FAMILY

In the early 1960s, James Stuart Walters along with wife Patricia Marie Shelly and two small girls, Shelly Marie and Mary Elizabeth moved into the home that was previously owned by Blake and Minerva Darling. The first known tenants were the Kriegers. The home is located directly across from Lakeville school. Soon after moving in, another daughter Cheryl Lynn and finally a son, Robert James was born. Jim worked for over 45 years and retired from Mansfield Sanitary at the Big Prairie branch as a Journeyman Tool and Die Maker. Jim also had his own business THE LAKE O'DELL GUN SHOP. It was located in the west side of his garage. Pat stayed at home until the children were older. She sold license plates out of the home for fifty cents a plate profit to make some extra money. Years later Pat worked as a secretary at Washington Mutual Insurance Company on County Road 100 until she retired. Jim and Pat built a new home in 1978 on County Road 100. They remained in this home till they both passed away in 2011.

Easter Sunday – 1968 or 1969

Daughter Shelly married Larry Spade in 1978. They have two children Bryan and Scott (Angela). She has three grandsons to complete the family. Mary was married to the late Richard Tipton. She has two children Rex and Michelle (Aaron). Mary has four grandchildren. Cheryl married Joe Fields and has two children, Nathan and Danny (Amanda). Cheryl is a grandmother of three. Bob married Brenda Shrock and they have 2 sons, Jesson and Eagan. – *Submitted by Cheryl Fields*

JOHN LEONARD WIGTON FAMILY

One of John and Sarah Wigton's eleven children was George Wigton. He was born in the house on the corner of SR 179 and SR 226, currently the home of Saundra Rhamey. George married Hazel Everly and they had a son, John Leonard (Jack). Jack was the father of Lynn, who married Richard Baker.

Lynn Wigton Baker

JOSEPH WIGTON FAMILY

Joseph Wigton, born in June 1779, was the son of William and Martha Wallace, both of Scotland. Martha was related to Sir William Wallace. Both died in Scotland. All the children, except Mary, came to America. Joseph Wigton married Sarah Porter in America. Carson P. Wigton, son of Joseph and Sarah, was born in 1835 and later married Menerva Anne Crooks.

My great-great-grandfather, Carson P. Wigton, lived in the Roseville and Zanesville, Ohio, area.

My great-grandfather, John Joseph Wigton, came to the Holmes County area and settled on a farm on State Route 179 near Nashville, Ohio. Later, he moved to the house on the corner of State Routes 179 and 226. John Joseph Wigton received a letter from Scotland stating he was heir to a Shire in Scotland, which was so much land. He would have had to go back to Scotland to claim the Shire and live on the land. He did not want to leave America so the land would go back to the government. John and Sarah Wigton had eleven children. John and some of his boys hauled logs with teams of horses. Later, he worked on the state highways from which he retired. He was a Sunday School teacher for a good many years at the Lakeville Methodist Church. A good many of his children lived in the Lakeville and surrounding areas.

My grandfather, James Edgar Wigton, married Nellie Shearer of Lakeville. They bought the house where Carl and Velma lived, across from the present post office. He worked for the Monitor Sad Iron Co. in Big Prairie most of his life. Edgar and Nellie Wigton had six children: Walter, Marjore, Martha, Carl, Harry, and Mary. All the children were born in Lakeville and graduated from Lakeville Special School.

My father, Carl Wigton, married Velma Carpenter in September of 1938. They had three children: Ronald, Donald, and Virginia. Carl Wigton worked at the Akron Brass, Flexible Co., Monitor Sad Iron, and custodian of the Lakeville School for many years until he died in July of 1978. He was interested in sports and coached softball teams in Lakeville. Carl was an All Star Player on the basketball team in the years of 1933, 1934, and 1935.

Ronald and Linda Wigton live near Lakeville and have two sons. Virginia married Denny Ogden and lives on Shreve Road, Wooster, Ohio, and has two sons. Donald married Sandy Burgett of Lakeville and lives in Lakeville. They have three children: Jarrod, Angela, and Stephanie. Donald worked at Mansfield Plumbing Products in Big Prairie. – *Submitted by Don Wigton to Holmes County Ohio to 1985*

ZANE WIGTON FAMILY

Zane Wigton was a nearly lifelong resident of Lakeville. Zane was the tenth of eleven children born to John and Sarah Wigton. He was born April 12, 1897 and married Golda Mosser (born January 18, 1899 in Ashland, OH) whom he met while working in an Ashland restaurant. Zane and Golda lived on a farm south of Lakeville. They had one daughter, Farrell, who attended school at Lakeville. She married John Brown and moved to Nashville. Zane and Golda were active in the Lakeville Methodist Church. Zane served on the Lakeville School Board of Education for a time. Zane and his brother, Charles, bought property between County Road 100 and the Lake O'Dell outlet. Zane and Golda built a garage to live in while building their house (current home of Daryl and Lisa Miller). Zane and Charlie divided the rest of the property into lots which were sold for summer cottages with some later becoming year-round residences. Zane was a carpenter for the remainder of his career. - *Submitted by Barb Long*

Left to Right: John Wigton, Sarah Wigton, Golda Wigton, Zane Wigton and Farrell Wigton in front.

FAMILIES ON TOWNSHIP ROAD 1060

On Twp Rd 1060, going in towards the hotel / lake, was the Horn and then the Wild home with the pond. Then Marian and Olin Olney who had the only well on the street. The rest of us had to go there and prime the pump then carry buckets of water to our homes for drinking, bathing, and laundry. The next home was Chuck and Lorna Bookman, then Pete, Mary, and Becky Moyer. The 5th house were Pattens who died of asphyxiation from a heater. Next was Cloyd Derrenberger. In the last home lived Mary, Dick, and Jacquie Gilliam. Across the road, up a hill from the Moyer house was the community out house. – *Submitted by Becky Moyer Darr*

MISCELLANEOUS SUBMITTED PICTURES

Babe Davenport

Herb Knox

Raymond "Buck" Knox

Joe Bock, Mary Moyer, Buck Knox

Raymond Kick

Marian Olney and her son, Olin.

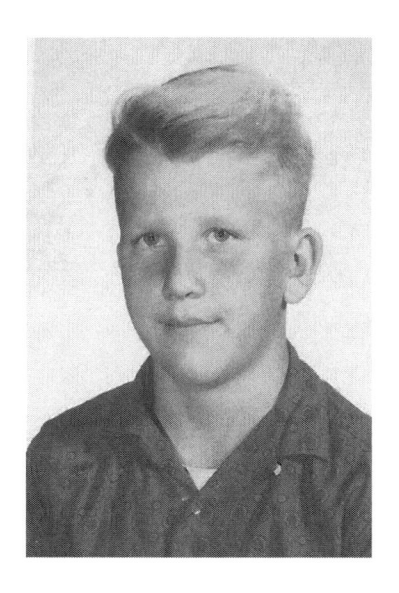

Dave Miller, son of Mark and Olive Miller and brother of Kathryn "Teenie" Mackey. Also pictured with Becky Moyer.

Standing – Martin J. Bray, Lem Greathouse, Clyde Collier, Asa Thompson, John R. Tope. Seated – Roscoe Deitch, Howard Rhamey, Halley Leyda, Dalley Rush

The Graber girls – Terra, Holly, Christine, and Samantha. They lived in the former home of John and Elsie Tope at the corner of Horseshoe Alley and St Rt 226

24

Lakeville Homes of the Past

The following pages are random old pictures and drawings of homes in Lakeville and the surrounding area. Do you recognize any of them?

House built by Joseph DeYarmon then owned by Kantzer

Thompson owned house behind Grocery Store built by DeYarmen

Same house as pictured above on left side.

RESIDENCE OF G. F. KANTZER

Main St. Lakeville, O.

The following pictures are from the Atlas of Holmes Co. Ohio 1875 and consist of farms that were located in the countryside surrounding Lakeville.

Handwritten note at bottom of picture was made by Vera Butler. She believed this picture might be the Carl Maurer farm.

Res. of **J.S. HUGHES**, Washington, Twp. Holmes Co. O. 1¼ Miles south of Lakeville. Farm of 224 Acres.

Carl Maurer ?

RES. OF DAVID SMETZER, WASHINGTON TW'P, HOLMES CO. O.
FARM OF 180 A.

Over the hills to Bonnett's Lake, Res. of JOHN SHOUP, Esq.
WASHINGTON TWP, HOLMES CO. O. FARM OF 425 A.

Dean Miller ?

Handwritten note at bottom of picture was made by Vera Butler. She believed this picture might be the current Dean Miller farm.

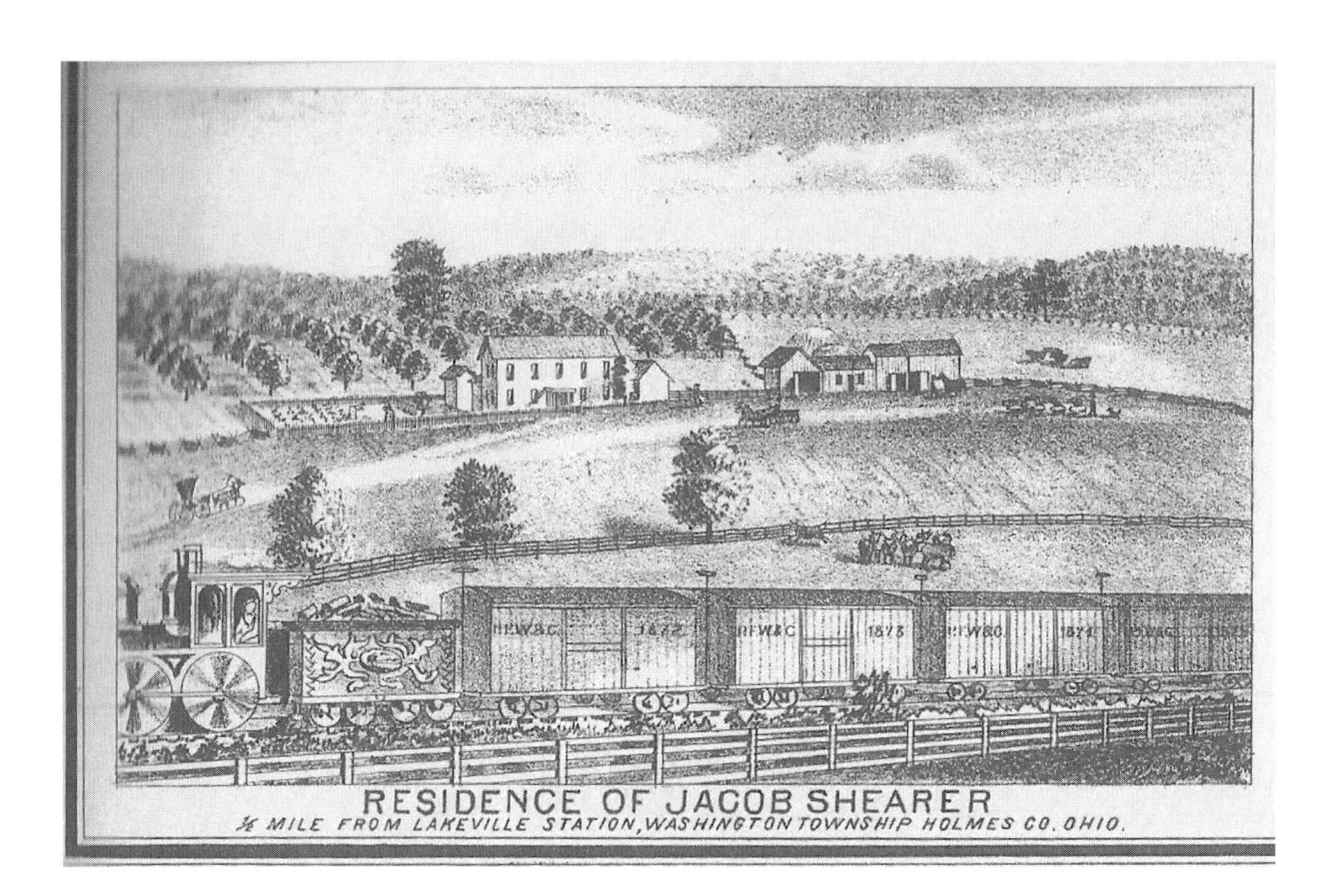

RESIDENCE OF JACOB SHEARER
½ MILE FROM LAKEVILLE STATION, WASHINGTON TOWNSHIP HOLMES CO. OHIO.

"BONNETT LAKE"   RES. OF ISAAC N. BONNETT.
FARM OF 154 ACRES IN WASHINGTON TOWNSHIP, HOLMES CO., OHIO.

FORMER RESIDENCE OF JAMES LIGGETT JR.

Residence of JAMES LIGGETT Jr. Washington Township, Holmes Co. Ohio.
1 MILE SOUTH OF LAKEVILLE.

References

Cooper, Courtney. (2014, August 14). *Odell's Lake*. Power Point presentation.

Cring Henry. (1875) *Caldwell's Atlas of Holmes Co. Ohio*. Condit, OH: J.A. Caldwell

Giet, Terry. (1994). *Holmes County A Pictorial History*. Orrville, OH: Spectrum Publications

Harris, Brooks and Kathleen. (2005). *Holmes County, Ohio – History in Photo Postcards*. Millersburg, OH: Tope Printing. Pictures published with written permission of Brooks Harris.

Holmes County Antique Festival Souvenir Book. (1978)

Holmes County Cemetery Index and Cemetery Locations – compilation located at Millersburg branch of Holmes County, Ohio, Library

Holmes County Heirs newsletter. Nov Dec 1989

Holmes County Heirs newsletter. Jan Feb 1992

Holmes County Historic Book Committee. (1985). *Holmes County Ohio to 1985*. Salem, WV: Walsworth Publishing

Holmes County Historical Society. (2002) *Holmes County Historical Sketches*. Sugarcreek, OH: Carlisle Printing

Holmes County – Old Schools, Early Churches – compilation located at Millersburg branch of Holmes County, Ohio, Library

Holmes County Recorder, The. – Dec 1978

Holmes County Veterans – compilation at Millersburg branch of Holmes County Library

Kopp, Paul. (1979) An account of his youth written for his daughter-in-law, Rita Kopp. Printed with written permission from Rita Kopp.

Stiffler, A.J. (1907). *The Standard Atlas of Holmes County Ohio*. Cincinnati, OH: The Standard Atlas Publishing Co.

The Trial Commencement Number 1925 – Holmes County School. 1925 Lakeville High School Year Book

Big Prairie / Lakeville High School / West Holmes High School Year Books. 1948 thru 1969

Findagrave.com website

Newspaper articles found online– authors unknown

(1858, December 23). Untitled. *Holmes County Republican*

(1860, March 22). Untitled. *Holmes County Republican*

(1880, January 22). Untitled. *The Democratic Press*

(1885, September 4). The Sherman Brigade Reunion, *The New York Times*

(1890, March 9). Untitled. *Stark County Democrat*

(1901, May 7). Lakeville Damaged $15,000. *Akron Daily Democrat*

(1901, August 9). From Holmes County. *Akron Daily Democrat*

Orchard, James. (1984) Lakeville Knows Its School is Special. *Daily Record*

DeGraw, Ed. (1984, February 29, 1984) Progressive Education in 1913. *Times Reporter*

Made in the USA
Monee, IL
28 June 2023